Confidence
—— in the ——
Classroom

D1337477

CONFIDENCE

IN THE

CLASSROOM

Realistic encouragement
for teachers

PHILIP R. MAY

*Reader in Education
University of Durham*

Inter-Varsity Press

INTER-VARSITY PRESS
38 De Montfort Street, Leicester LE1 7GP, England

Unless otherwise stated, Scripture quotations in this publication are
from the Holy Bible, New International Version, copyright © 1973,
1978, 1984 by the International Bible Society, and published in Great
Britain by Hodder & Stoughton Ltd.

First published 1988

British Library Cataloguing in Publication Data

May, Philip R. (Philip Radford), *1928–*
    Confidence in the classroom : realistic
    encouragement for teachers.
    1. Education – Christian viewpoints
    I. Title
    261

ISBN 0–85110–834–2

Set in Linotron Times 10 on 12pt
Typeset in Great Britain by Input Typesetting Ltd, London

Printed in Great Britain by Cox & Wyman Ltd, Reading

*Inter-Varsity Press is the book-publishing division of the
Universities and Colleges Christian Fellowship
(formerly the Inter-Varsity Fellowship), a student
movement linking Christian Unions in universities and
colleges throughout the United Kingdom and the Republic
of Ireland, and a member movement of the International
Fellowship of Evangelical Students. For information
about local and national activities write to UCCF, 38
De Montfort Street, Leicester LE1 7GP.*

Contents

Introduction

The other evening I was chatting to a Christian teenager about his faith and life as a Christian. At one point, we got on to his schooldays. He didn't enjoy them much. 'It was a non-event for most of us,' he said. A typical, sweeping, adolescent generalization, you might think. School did not seem to have made much impact on him. So how do teachers, especially Christian teachers, have real influence in their schools? I know at least two in Keith's old school. How do they witness to their faith, to what they know really matters for their pupils?

Of course, the job for which teachers are employed is not to preach at all, but to teach the subjects and skills they are qualified to teach. That's what they are paid for. So how do Christian teachers fulfil the calling of every Christian to proclaim Christ in all aspects of their life and work? And in particular, how do they do this when professional morale is low, when they work with disillusioned colleagues, in unattractive surroundings, with inadequate resources, disruptive pupils, and for a local authority whose educational views they regard with suspicion and distrust?

That was a question I never thought to ask until I'd been teaching for several years. Despite a church upbringing, I did not become a Christian until I left university and had been teaching for over two years. Even after that great event, I went on as before at school. Looking back, I don't think I realized for quite some time that the Lord wanted me to apply my faith – and His teaching – to *all* aspects of my work and life. I could see how I might do this in out-of-school activities. But how should it affect my teaching of English? I didn't know.

I've since found out that lots of other Christian teachers have exactly the same problem. One of them summed it up for me very helpfully. I'd like to quote him at length, because he makes a number of points which I know many other Christians who teach also need to hear. I'd gone to see him and his Christian teacher wife at their home, and we got on to the subject of witnessing. This is what he said:

> For a long time Jenny and I found it hard to know what our role as Christians really was. We attend a very active church. Many members are busy with church activities, and some go out from the church to minister and evangelize. We did a bit to help but not much. We weren't sure what God wanted of us. Some of the church members thought we should teach in the Sunday school, and help with the youth club. Just because we were teachers, that's what was expected of us.
>
> But we didn't feel that was right. After all, teaching's hard work, and when the weekend comes, we

want a change and rest like everyone else. We didn't feel we could give out all week, prepare every night, and then give out still more at the weekend. But we felt really guilty that we were not doing more in the church.

You see, for us, work was just work, and church was where you worked for Christ. But God has shown us how wrong we were to think like that. He showed us that where He wanted us to work for Him was in school, not so much at church. Now we understand that we express and live out our Christianity more at work than anywhere else. So now we are more our Christian selves naturally at school than anywhere else except home.

It's taken us a long time to realize this. We don't want to be self-conscious Christians – I mean witnessing in a deliberate, self-conscious way, putting on this activity, doing that job, like in church. We want to be Christ-conscious Christians, trusting Him to lead us into His will and purpose. And we are that in school, just doing our job every day as well as we can. In that way, we are actually missionaries in school.

So at last we feel free. Free to be real persons. A lot of Christians in church, as well as Christian teachers, need to be educated about this. We need to free each other from our worldly, or our cultural, expectations of one another – 'You're a teacher, so you do the teaching in church.' Now we are free from these pressures. They're still there in the attitudes of some church members. But we are free, free to be real persons for Christ at last.

At this point we started to discuss what we meant by freedom in Christ, but John soon returned to their work in their schools. I'd like you to read just a little more of what he said. I think it's both helpful and moving.

Since we arrived at this understanding, things at school have really come alive for us both. We don't have to engineer situations in which we can speak about Christ. God brings them up naturally, and we can respond in the same way. You see, we don't always know what to do. Nor do we know what we bring into situations.

When you manipulate situations, you often fail to see the real opportunities God has prepared for you. You even prevent them happening. We don't know when to go fast or slow. We just have to trust in God and let Him lead. We have to stop being self-conscious, so we can allow God to let Christ be realized in us unconsciously. We used to think we were taking the Lord with us into school. Now we know He's there already, and we just have to follow Him in there.

I think that's a terrific testimony. I just wish I'd heard it when I was a new Christian teacher – though I might well not have fully understood what he was saying then. But I agree with him 100%. If you're a Christian whose job is to teach in school, that's where God most wants you to work for Him, not anywhere else. And that's a full-time commitment.

You may still want something that applies directly to your daily teaching life. That's certainly what I needed when I worked full-time in schools. My burning conviction is that God's Word is vitally and excitingly relevant to everything you do as a teacher. Therefore I've tried to share personally with you at the practical, down-to-earth, everyday, classroom level. Although I now work in a university, and have done for twenty-eight years – I'm even, to my surprise, the most senior member of

10

my department – I'm basically a teacher. I care about children and my students. I care about my colleagues. I want with all my heart that my fellow Christians who teach should do what I try to do (in stumbling fashion, I confess) – apply God's Word to the classroom.

Let me ask you a question. What's your top priority as a teacher? Of all the aims and hopes you have, which comes number one on the list? Why not stop reading and write your answer down on a piece of paper? I think you may find it helpful as we go along. I'm going to quote a lot from practising Christian teachers in this book. I've got some of their answers to my question here. When you've decided on yours, have a look at theirs.

Ready now? How does your answer compare with these?

- To get my marking done. (That's an English teacher who says she always has too much written work to mark.)
- To help my students get through their examinations successfully.
- To control my ten-year-olds.
- To make sure the drama group has enough practice to do a good performance.
- To teach my kids well and care for them.
- To make my subject enjoyable for as many pupils as I can.
- To survive to the end of term.

I don't know about you, but I think there's something to agree with in every one of those suggestions. I'm sure I'd like yours too. And if you flick through the pages of most books on education, you'll have a whole lot more. Put together, they remind me of that highly complicated road system outside Birmingham known as Spaghetti

Junction. Once on it, you find roads going in every direction. It really is rather like a plate of spaghetti. You need all your wits about you to find the exit you want. Reading lots of aims in education can have the same effect.

But of course, for the Christian teacher, I've really asked the wrong question, haven't I? Certainly, you've got to have your priorities sorted out. But the truly important question for Christians who teach is this: What is God's top priority for you as a teacher? I think Paul supplied the answer in his second letter to Timothy, where he writes:

> *Do your best to present yourself to God as one approved, a workman who does not need to be ashamed and who correctly handles the word of truth (2 Timothy 2:15).*

There's a great ideal for you. Approved by God. A workman who is not ashamed. One who rightly opens out and handles God's Word. Don't you think that sums up the challenge that God gives you, as a Christian in the classroom? I know that unless you teach RE, you probably don't teach the Bible in your lessons. This verse means much more than that. As a Christian you *must* handle His Word faithfully, with understanding and authority. You have to live it out, every day. It needs to permeate all your thoughts and all your speaking with its purity and truth.

For, Christian teacher, wherever you are employed, you are first and foremost teaching for Christ. He's put you where you are right now for just that purpose. So I invite you to come with me. Let's search the Scriptures together, and apply them by the guidance of the Spirit of truth Himself to our life and work as teachers for the Lord. I guarantee it'll make a difference to you. You'll be challenged. You'll be excited. Even if, like many teachers today, you've experienced failure and defeat, or feel you're getting nowhere, you'll be thrilled to realize afresh what God has called you to do, and to see again how He helps you to do it. And one result of this really can be confidence in the classroom.

— 1 —

Being a witness

I wonder if you've ever been inside a court of law when different cases are being tried. Lots of cases that are tried there are straightforward, especially if the defendant pleads guilty from the start. If, however, the plea is one of not guilty, then the whole business takes much longer because the prosecution has to prove its case. And they'll have a much better chance of convincing the judge and jury, or the magistrates, if they can produce one or more witnesses to back up their claims. The defence also needs to supply witnesses if it can, to support the defendant's plea. But it quite often happens that an accused person comes to court, pleads not guilty, but has no-one at all to call in his defence. Such a person has a real problem, and so, sometimes, have those who have to decide the case, especially when one side has several witnesses and the other has none, but is genuinely telling the truth as he or she sees it.

Just picture the scene. There's been some trouble

down town one night, with groups of youths fighting. One young man, eighteen-year-old Jerry Baker, was apprehended by the police and is now in court accused of a breach of the peace. The prosecution says he was there at the time, and was actually caught running away from the scene. Worse still, two witnesses swear that they saw him fighting, and a policeman testifies that, when he caught him, his jacket was torn and his breath smelled of alcohol.

Now it's Jerry's turn to tell his side of the story. He's pleaded not guilty. Yes, he was there at the time. He'd been to a film show with a friend and had gone to a pub for a drink before going home. When he came out of the pub, he found himself in the middle of a crowd of youths bent on trouble. One tried to grab him and pulled his jacket as he turned to run away. He did not swing a punch or start fighting. He just tried to get away as quickly as he could. He'd been in trouble before with the police and did not want to be found on the scene this time.

Now it so happens that he's telling the truth. But, unlike the prosecution, he has no witnesses to back up his story, because his friend had gone home earlier. All he can say is that it was dark, and in the confusion it would be easy for casual witnesses to make a mistake. He did not see the witnesses there. All he did was try to leave the scene as quickly as possible.

You see Jerry's problem? Well, it's even worse, because he's not a bright lad or very articulate. So the prosecutor makes him look foolish and confuses him during the cross-examination. Yet he *is* telling the truth. So what is the court to decide? All the evidence appears to favour the prosecution. If only Jerry's friend had stayed with him, or he'd been able to find someone there at the time who could say that Jerry had not been involved in the fighting. If only he had a reliable witness!

Such a witness is a pretty important character, whether his evidence is oral or written. What he is saying to those who have called him, or who have come to listen to him, is this: 'These facts are genuine.' 'What this person says is the truth, and my testimony proves it.' 'I was there, and I saw it with my own eyes.' 'This is what happened to me.' And so on. He may be testifying that a certain transaction did take place, that he witnessed a signature on some legal document, or that he heard someone say something. In court, he swears to tell the truth, the whole truth, and nothing but the truth. But wherever a witness is testifying, those who hear him or her are asked to believe that what they are being told is right, accurate, and to be relied upon.

The witness is not there to recount what somebody else experienced or said had taken place. Such information might be very interesting. But it would not be accepted in a court of law, for instance, where hearsay evidence, as this second-hand reporting is called, is not admissible. Even if it were accepted, it would not really help very much because its reliability could not be guaranteed, as the testimony of a truthful witness can be. For a witness is someone who was there at the time, or who knows from personal experience, what he or she is talking about.

The biblical view of witnessing

Now, as anyone knows who reads the New Testament, all Christians are called to be witnesses, to bear testimony to the Lord Jesus Christ and to their faith in Him. Don't imagine it's a job for a specialist, someone who has been specially trained, an expert of some kind, one who has been set apart by the church especially for this duty. You might well be tempted to think like that, because I'm sure that's what the world thinks. What happens when your car needs repairing or the roof needs mending? What do you do when you find that you've to sell your house and move to a new area? Most of us automatically turn to the professionals to do the job for us. We live in an age when we naturally look to specialists to help out in much of the business of living.

But that's not what to do where Christianity is concerned. It's not just apostles, or prophets, or pastors, or teachers, or church elders, who are witnesses. If you are a Christian, then you have to witness to that fact wherever you live, wherever you work, whatever you do, no matter how old or young you are or what background you have come from.

What's that you say? *You* couldn't witness in public to your faith? You're not like so-and-so who's so attractive, and has such a gift for speaking, especially about personal things. *You* didn't have the special theological education which helps with this sort of thing. You've always been shy. You are not one who is pushy or likes the limelight. And anyway, situations differ and you would not always know what to say or how to say it. You're perfectly OK with your normal school work, but this is different.

Yes, I know, and I accept all that you are telling me. I know that you are just a very ordinary, straightforward, simple person who likes to get on with living in a quiet, unobtrusive way. Of course you go to church regularly, and you read your Bible and say your prayers every day. You just try to get on with your life and to be a good Christian. That's hard enough for anyone, these days.

I sympathize with you. The thought of being a witness – *me* being a witness – is a bit scary for most of us. We don't want to be in the spotlight at the front of the stage. We don't like to draw too much attention to ourselves. After all, we're not that important, are we? Oh yes, we'll do our best, but behind the scenes, please. We might even agree, if we're really pressed, to be the serving-maid, the butler or the messenger. You know, the bit parts. But one of the lead actors? Oh no, that's not for us.

Just think of Jerry Baker again for a minute. Remember he was accused of an offence of which he was innocent. Two people said they saw him fighting, but we know they were mistaken. Jerry has no-one to witness for him. Nobody will get up in court and support his side of things. The court has only his word against that of several on the prosecution side. I have to tell you from my experience as a magistrate that Jerry's chances of acquittal are not good. Well, how would you judge a case like that?

Let's also think of your situation. In a way, the Lord Jesus Christ is on trial there. Are you going to speak up for Him? You know He's innocent too. But he needs someone to present His case in your school, your staff-room, your classroom, your out-of-school activities with children and young people, with the head teacher, or the parent-teacher association. Never mind at this stage about *how* to present His case. We'll come to that later. That's what this book is largely about, to help with this presentation problem. The Lord Jesus needs you as a witness. What are His chances if you keep quiet, or back off altogether? Like Jerry Baker's, perhaps?

Don't answer that question yet. Save it till you've read a whole lot more of the book. Till you've examined more of the evidence. Especially the biblical evidence. And to do that, let's begin from the most realistic point of view we know. Not yours. Not mine. But God's viewpoint. That means I'm encouraging you (and myself) to go straight to the Bible and see what God has to say on the subject of witnessing. You'll find that He stresses at least four features which are characteristic of a Christian witness.

18

Called by God

The first one is that every witness for Christ has been called to that work by God Himself. One of the most important things that Jesus said towards the end of His earthly ministry can be found in chapter 24 of Matthew's Gospel. In verse 14 we read:

And this gospel of the kingdom will be preached in the whole world as a testimony [for a witness] *to all nations, and then the end will come.*

Did you notice how the Lord Jesus phrased that statement? He was setting out the facts to tell us exactly what is going to happen. Not what might be, but what *is*. The gospel *will be* preached. It will be preached *in all the world*. It will be preached *to all nations*. And it will be preached *as a testimony*, a witness. And then the end will come.

Those are facts. The King of glory says so. So that's settled. The gospel of the kingdom has got to be preached. That means that someone's got to do it. And to all people everywhere.

There are more facts to come. The Bible tells us that every Christian is God's workmanship (Ephesians 2:10), selected and separated out by God Himself. 'You . . . were dead in your trespasses and sins . . . But . . . God . . . made us alive with Christ' (Ephesians 2:1–4). 'Now in Christ Jesus you who once were far away, have been brought near through the blood of Christ' (Ephesians 2:13). As Christ told His disciples in the upper room: 'You did not choose me, but I chose you . . . to go and bear fruit' (John 15:16). He went on to say this: 'The Spirit of truth . . . will testify about me. And you also must testify, for you have been with me from the beginning' (John 15:26–27). It is not simply a case of

19

God Himself bearing witness, through the Person and work of the Holy Spirit. 'You also must testify,' He says to His followers. And don't forget to whom he was talking. There were one or two educated ones listening, but most of the disciples were humble, unlettered fishermen, 'unschooled, ordinary men' as Luke describes them in Acts 4:13.

What's that I hear you say? You accept all that. But Jesus was talking to His disciples, to the specially selected eleven (Judas Iscariot had left them for ever by this time). That's true. So let's move to the account of Christ's ascension into heaven at the beginning of the Acts of the Apostles. This event was witnessed by many more than the eleven, and it was to all of them, and so to all Christians down the ages thereafter, that Jesus said:

> *You will receive power when the Holy Spirit comes on you; and you will be my witnesses in Jerusalem, and in all Judea and Samaria, and to the ends of the earth (Acts 1:8).*

You will be my witnesses – all of you. Not just the apostles. All of us. That 'you' means you. It means me. It means every Christian who has ever lived. So if you are a Christian, you know this fact. Whatever else God wants you to do for Him, He has called you to be a witness. In the courtroom of life, He has nominated you to give evidence on His behalf.

An imperative task

The second main truth about Christian witnessing is that every Christian is *commanded* to do it. The Lord does not merely ask us to witness, or to consider the idea as a possible option which some of us might like to take up. None of us has any choice in the matter. 'This gospel of the kingdom *will be* preached in the whole world.' 'You also *must testify*.' 'You *shall* be my witnesses.' It's sometimes possible to escape being a witness in court. But there is clearly no escape from such a responsibility for any of the people of God. Those excuses we were making look pretty feeble beside such authoritative instructions, especially when you remember who it is who's giving them.

In any case, it's inevitable that witnessing for Christ can't be left just to certain selected individuals in each generation. I mean, think about the task we've been given. God says He wants the gospel preached in the *whole* world and to *all* nations. His witnesses must go 'to the ends of the earth'. The end won't come till every group of people in every corner of the world has heard the good news of Jesus Christ. As Paul asked in his letter to the Romans, 'How shall they hear without someone preaching to them?' (Romans 10:14). Unless every Christian is prepared to be a witness to those close at hand, and unless some are prepared to go to distant places with the message of Christ, some people may never learn about the gospel of the kingdom. As far as they are concerned, the Lord Jesus will have lost His case. Therefore we must all testify in the place to which God has called us.

Equipped by God

I know a teacher who was once accused by the police of a certain misdemeanour. He knew the case would come to court, and so he came to ask me what he should do. I told him what the court procedure would be like, and he then told me his story. He was to be prosecuted for alleged shoplifting. He said it was all a horrible mistake and that he was not guilty. On what he told me

21

I thought he stood a reasonable chance of being acquitted. It would not be easy and he would certainly have to go into the witness box and be subjected to cross-examination. In the end, he pleaded guilty and was fined. The case was not reported in the press. That was one thing he had been afraid of. He knew there was more chance of the case being reported if he had pleaded not guilty. But what he had most feared was having to give evidence. I pleaded with him to do this. After all, for one who believed himself innocent, to plead guilty is dreadful. But for him the ordeal was too great to face. As he kept saying to me, 'I know I'm supposed to be an educated man, but I know that when I have to go into that box, I'll go to pieces because I just won't know what to say.'

Two Bible examples

The Bible has a number of stories of people whom God called to be witnesses but who, like that poor teacher, and perhaps like you and me as well, were most reluctant to undertake the task. Two of the most famous were Moses and Jeremiah. They both made what they thought were powerful excuses as to why they should not speak out for God. I think you'll find it very instructive to see how God dealt with them, because it underlines very strongly the third feature of Christian witnessing.

Moses

Moses was especially reluctant. He had lots of reasons why he should not be a witness for God. You'll find them in Exodus chapters 3–4. How familiar they all sound.

He began with the fact that, in his opinion, he was totally unsuitable. 'Who am I, that I should go to Pharaoh and bring the Israelites out of Egypt?' (3:11).

22

I reckon most of us would feel like that when faced with that sort of challenge. But look at God's reply. He directs Moses' (and our) attention away from self to God. He said: 'I will be with you'(3:12). You'll not be on your own, Moses. I'll be there as well, all the time. There's no answer to that. So Moses shifted his ground. Now he said he was afraid that the Israelites would want him to identify more specifically the God he represented. So God at once revealed His most special name, telling Moses: 'Say to the Israelites: "I AM has sent me to you" '(3:14).

'But', answered Moses, 'what if they do not believe me or listen to me?' (4:1). Now this is another very common excuse. Haven't you used it sometimes? I have. But, you know, it's stupid, because it misses the whole point about being a witness. The witness's job is to speak the truth fully, and as clearly and openly as possible. That's all. He or she is not responsible in any way for how the witnessing is received by those who hear it or see it. Certainly we have to think about what we are going to say and do, and how we'll say and do it. We also have to think about our audience – who and what kind of people they are. But when you witness, you simply have to do the best you can, as faithfully as you can. You are not answerable for what happens next. The onus is then upon those who were listening. If they refuse to believe you, or if they close their ears to your message, that's sad. But it's their problem, not yours. They'll have to answer for how they respond, not you. So this excuse of Moses? Forget it.

God overlooked it too. He went on encouraging Moses, this time by performing some miracles which He then empowered Moses also to perform if necessary. But Moses was still not finished. He now tried another tack. He told God that he was a very inadequate speaker, one who had never been eloquent. 'I am slow

23

of speech and tongue', he said (4:10). Have you heard that one before? I bet you have. It's another very common excuse that many Christians make. So take special notice of the Lord's reply. I reckon every Christian, and Christian teachers most of all, should learn it by heart, and think about it often.

Who gave man his mouth? Who makes him deaf or dumb? Who gives him sight or makes him blind? Is it not I, the Lord? Now go; I will help you speak and will teach you what to say (4:11–12).

What he said to Moses, He says to you and me as well. Why should we be afraid or unwilling to speak out for our Lord? After all, He gave us the power of speech when He created us, and He will not only teach us what to say and do for Him in any situation, but will help us in the actual witnessing itself. So what is there to worry about? All we have to do is to trust Him, and obey.

Even after all this, Moses pleaded with God to send someone else. God refused, but He did assure Moses that his brother Aaron would act as his mouthpiece. But Moses still had to go. He still had to witness. So have you, and so have I. God has issued us with a subpoena which we ignore at our peril.

Jeremiah

Jeremiah's chief excuse was that he was too young to do what God was asking. God reassured him that he must go, but there was no need to be afraid because 'I am with you and will rescue you,' declares the Lord (Jeremiah 1:8). And He immediately put His words into Jeremiah's mouth and prepared him for his mission. Youthfulness was, and is, no barrier at all where God is concerned. Remember the young and timid Timothy. Paul wrote of him that he had made a 'good confession

24

in the presence of witnesses' (1 Timothy 6:12). Like Paul himself, whom Jesus appointed 'as a servant and as a witness of what you have seen of me and what I will show you' (Acts 26:16), Timothy testified to his faith before many people, despite his age and disposition.

Let's now return to that eighth verse in Acts, chapter 1. The secret of every successful witnessing to God is clearly revealed there. God never calls you to do anything for Him without preparing you properly first. That's as true about witnessing as anything else. Remember the promise that God made again and again to His chosen servants in the Old Testament days – 'I will be with you.' It's echoed again and again by Christ to His followers, as in 'Surely, I am with you always' (Matthew 28:20). Here that promise is explained. 'You will receive power when the Holy Spirit comes on you', says Christ to all who turn to Him.

So it's absolutely useless for you and me to say that we can't witness for the Lord, because God has given us the resources to do it, the moment we become Christians. He puts His Spirit within us. And it is His Spirit, not ours, that enables us to confess that Jesus Christ is Lord. We don't have to be afraid of anything or anyone, including ourselves. If we trust Him – and that's the key to the whole business – God will give us the right words to say at the right time. You know that you can ask for anything in Christ's name, and Christ will do it for you (John 14:14; 16:24). Look how His power transformed fearful, dispirited disciples into men of authority and boldness who could say fearlessly and with full assurance, as Peter did before the formidable Sanhedrin, 'We are witnesses of these things' (Acts 5:32).

Isn't that super. And exciting. I reckon one of the most encouraging facts about Christian witnessing is that God always equips you for the task. So don't be afraid. Hold on to God's promise. And when you go into court tomorrow, speak up and act out your faith. Don't just sit back and keep quiet. As I heard Don Petry, formerly of CBN University, say once at a Christian educators' convention in Washington DC, you've got to rest on the promises, not on the premises.

Personal witnessing is to Christ

So that's three features of Christian witnessing that the Bible stresses. Every Christian witness is called, commanded and equipped by God. The fourth characteristic concerns what we witness about – or, more correctly, Whom we witness about. No witness ever speaks primarily about himself or herself. In the law court, they do have to say something about themselves – who they are, where they live, why they are qualified to be witnesses in the case in question, and so on. But primarily, a witness is there on someone else's behalf. He's speaking for that person and supporting that person's testimony.

The Christian, of course, is witnessing for Christ. 'You will be *my* witnesses', says Jesus (Acts 1:8). He appointed Paul 'as a witness of what you have seen *of me*'. As the Spirit of truth would 'testify about me', so must the disciples. And so must we. All our witnessing should point to Christ and away from ourselves. It is His gospel, His teaching, His saving work, His empowering and upholding, His coming again in judgment, His nature and will that we are to speak about and direct people towards.

Even so, the witnessing must also be a personal matter. The disciples were to testify about Christ, 'because they had been with him from the beginning'. Ananias told Paul that he was to be a witness to everyone of what *he* had seen and heard (Acts 22:15). John began his first letter by stressing that we speak what we know, what we have seen, heard and touched. The same applies to you and me. And to every other Christian, no matter where we live or work. A witness speaks from personal experience. That's where the value of his testimony lies.

And the power. It's because you know the Lord Jesus personally, and because you are able to experience His power and presence in your life every day, that you can testify truly and with confidence. Your task is to witness to what you know. Oh yes, I'm well aware that, like me, you need to know the Lord much more thoroughly and deeply. I also know that He still has a great deal to teach you (and me) about Himself. He knows that too. But He still calls you to witness in life and word about what you have learned and experienced of Him. The more you trust Him and draw closer to Him, the more you'll have to testify about, in your daily appearance on the witness stand.

Let me use a human illustration. I guess that if I asked you about Prince Charles you could tell me quite a lot about him. For instance, what he looks like, what family he has, what his background is, what some of his interests are. But I know someone who has actually met the Prince and talked with him on several occasions. Now if I ask *him* about Prince Charles, I'm sure he could tell me all that you can tell me. But he could add a whole lot more. After all, he's been in his company, shaken his hand, stood beside him, perhaps even smelt his aftershave. He's exchanged ideas and ordinary chat with him. So he *knows*, in a way that you don't know. You can imagine how much more convincing *his* answers to my questions will therefore be. The more time he's spent with the Prince, the more effective and authoritative his testimony about him will be. Isn't that just the same with us Christians, when we speak about our Lord?

Having got this far, you might now be asking how all

this applies to Christian teachers in their daily life and work with children and young people. That's what we're going to look at in the rest of the book, if you'll stick with me. First, though, I'd like to mention just three more general points about being a witness. I hope you'll agree that to be clear in our minds about them will help as we think about the Christian in school.

Three more facts about witnessing

First of all, a witness is always someone who is in the public eye. He has to be clearly identifiable. In a court of law, his first duty is to give his full name and address, and his occupation, if any. In a sense, he is on show to others. In the Christian's case, that means always. This is true of a witness even when the witnessing is of the silent kind. You must have seen reports of some solemn band of people who, without saying a word, march round and round outside, say, a foreign embassy, as a mark of concern for some suffering individual or group. Or the person who stations himself outside a court of justice to witness to his belief in the innocence of some accused or convicted man or woman. Or even the dog that sits on guard beside his master's grave, long after the funeral is over. The point is that, whether vocal or silent, whether by actions or words, these witnesses are out in the open, to be seen by others.

No Christian is to hide his or her light under a bowl. We have to put our light on a stand so that it can give light to everyone in the house (Matthew 5:15). How will folk be able to praise our Father in heaven if we do not let our light shine before them? As you know, the verse I'm alluding to here reminds us that we witness by our good deeds as well as by what we say.

And what you *are* also acts as a clear witness to the Lord. When you became a Christian, you became a new creature. It's important that those people with whom you come in contact really see the new person that you have become.

Many years ago, I used to teach in a school where there was a science teacher on the staff who was popular with very few of the other teachers. I don't know what he was like in the classroom and his laboratory. As far as I know, he was a competent teacher. He seemed to get on all right with his students, and some of them used to do very well in their examinations. But a lot of us in the staffroom did not like him. He had a sharp tongue and did not tolerate inefficiency in others. We younger ones were a bit afraid of him. When I left the school, naturally I lost touch with him and many others on the staff. But recently, I met one of those former colleagues who told me that this man had become a Christian and the difference was remarkable.

It is good and right to let people see how God is moulding us into the likeness of Christ. This is not a self-conscious parading of self in our character and our deeds. But it does mean that we have got to be consistent, and to act consistently, when open to view as well as in the privacy of those rooms of ours where others are not likely to be present.

This fact raises a very real problem for every Christian teacher, especially those who teach in the maintained schools or other secular institutions. The problem is summed up by a former Christian student of mine, now teaching in a comprehensive school, who wrote to me on the matter in the following terms.

I am a teacher, not a preacher. My job is to instruct my boys and girls in that area of knowledge and in those skills in which I am specially qualified. I am not there either to indoctrinate or to proselytize. [That's true, even if he were teaching in a specifically Christian establishment.] *So if I'm openly testifying to Christ in my school, am I not guilty of conditioning or brainwashing those I teach in order to produce not educated, independent, responsible young adults – which is what I'm expected to be doing – but mere converts to my own set of beliefs? Am I not also, since I teach in a state school, guilty of breaking the law concerning religious teaching if I speak openly about Jesus?*

The answer to both these questions is a resounding 'No'. In the first place, letting your colleagues and students know that you are a Christian is not indoctrinating, conditioning or brainwashing. It's just being open and honest. You do it simply, quietly and briefly without any fuss or over-insistence. Children are, in any case, always asking their teacher, 'What do you think, Sir/Miss?' We should tell them when they ask. Then no true teacher aims to produce docile, uncritical and passive acceptance of anything he or she teaches. We want all our pupils to learn to think for themselves, to question, ponder and discover, and to come to their own conclusions. It is the Christian teachers most of all who, remembering their Creator, recognize and defend the dignity and supreme worth of all children. So, as I told my former student, simply to let your children know where you stand in no way forces them to adopt your beliefs. Nor does it contravene English law.

Think of the greatest teacher of all time, Christ Himself. There has never been any teacher in the history of the world as totally committed to particular beliefs and a specific way of life as He. His hearers all knew this. Yet He never compelled anyone against their will to adopt His way of thinking and acting. All were free to accept or reject Him as they chose. I believe that His example is therefore a great encouragement to every teacher.

For it is impossible not to be yourself whatever you do and whatever you believe. We are what we are, the Christian teacher obviously so. No teacher is or can ever be entirely neutral. We all demonstrate what we are every day, in our words, gestures, facial expressions, actions, teaching methods, in class and outside, in the staffroom and the playgrounds around the school. And anyway, no Christian is expected, as a teacher, to go against or to deny the standards and beliefs which are central to his or her faith. You may have no chance at all during lessons to speak about Christ, and, even if an opportunity did come, you might not feel it right to take it. You might well prefer to wait until you could say a personal word after lessons end, to particular individuals. But you still witness by being a good professional, by loving your pupils, by preparing your work thoroughly, by maintaining good discipline and right standards, by being utterly reliable, by doing your marking and other duties as promptly as possible, by being there when needed, not to win favour when the head's eye is on you, but 'wholeheartedly, as if you were serving the Lord' (Ephesians 6:5–7).

There will be right opportunities to speak of your faith, to your colleagues and to some at least of your students. And I cannot emphasize too strongly that I am not here picturing you standing before your classes and preaching to them. They are a captive audience, there because they have to be there, and whether you teach them in a maintained or a private Christian school, I am totally opposed to any Christian teacher using such a method as a means of witnessing to them, especially when they have come to your lessons to study science, or literature, or mathematics, or music, or whatever else you are employed to teach them. Even so, you are a witness to Christ all the time in everything you do, not by pressurizing people but by being what you are, a

31

child of God, serving Him and your fellow humans.

I said there were three final points to make about being a witness, and we've noted the first, that a witness is a public figure. The second is that a witness is never the principal character in the drama, and we must never fall into the trap of thinking he is.

Such a temptation is ever present, and very easy to yield to. Imagine you see a road accident, and you are asked to appear in court as a witness. The day arrives at last. You've been getting ready for it for a while, thinking what you will say and how you will answer the questions you may be asked. Always you are conscious that the time is drawing nearer and nearer. You get up that morning and prepare extra carefully. You cannot go to your workplace or do your usual chores because you have to be in court by ten o'clock. So you go to the court and wait to be called. Suddenly you hear your name called by the court usher. In you go. You are the centre of attention. All eyes are on you as you take the oath and prepare to speak.

It's so very easy, under such pressure, to think too much of yourself and what you have to say, and so forget that you are not the main character but only a witness. Have you ever been asked to speak about your faith at a meeting, in someone's home perhaps, or in church, or even at a conference? If so, I'm sure you'll know the temptation to concentrate on yourself and on the effect you are having. Or perhaps on the way you are presenting your message. Anyway, not on the Lord, who is the real subject of the talk. No, no, no, let's never forget. Christ is always the only character about whom the Christian witnesses.

Lastly, for the third final point about witnessing, let's look at the word translated 'witness' throughout the New Testament. It's the Greek word *martys*, from which we get the English word 'martyr'. My dictionary defines a martyr as one who undergoes death or suffering for any great cause. It's a real reminder that being a witness for Christ can involve suffering. In fact we know, on Christ's own authority, and from His own constant experience on earth, that sooner or later every Christian who witnesses will have to endure hardship and suffering. It is a marvellous privilege to be able to speak and act for the King of kings and Lord of lords, a privilege that far outweighs the discomfort and the persecution that may follow such open testimony. But you and I should not forget that witnessing may well involve pain and self-denial, and we should be prepared for such consequences.

Any witness in court has to undergo cross-examination, usually by both prosecution and defence. That is never easy, and it can be horrid. The side for which you are speaking will be kindly and encouraging, and will help you to make your points as effectively as possible. But the other side is likely to try to cast doubt on all you say, or try to confuse you and make you appear unreliable or foolish. For lots of witnesses, their time in court is fairly straightforward. But to be on the witness stand can be a very testing and uncomfortable experience.

If this thought makes you fearful – and it's not one I much like either – then we should both turn our eyes upon Jesus, as the lovely chorus urges us to do. Remember that He too was a witness to the Father and of the gospel of the kingdom. He was, and is, as the book of Revelation reminds us, 'the faithful witness' (Revelation 1:5), and the 'faithful and true witness, the ruler of God's creation' (Revelation 3:14). As we do this, 'the things of earth will grow strangely dim', and we shall be uplifted and strengthened for our task of witnessing to and for our Lord and Saviour, the King of glory.

For prayer and discussion

1. Look up Hebrews 11:1 – 12:3, and meditate on the examples of witnessing listed there.

2. Make a list of all the reasons you may have for not wanting to witness openly to your faith. Pray about each one and examine yourself to discover why you feel as you do. If you can, share your reasons with other Christians, and discuss ways in which you all might overcome these difficulties.

3. When did you last speak to someone about Christ? Write down five (or ten) recent examples of your own personal experience with Jesus. Again, by yourself and with others, decide how you might share these examples (a) with another Christian; (b) with a non-Christian.

4. Discuss with others some of the possible different kinds of responses a Christian might encounter when witnessing (for example, interest, misunderstanding, hostility, scorn, concern, indifference, *etc.*). How might such knowledge assist you when preparing for future witnessing?

2

Profile of a Christian teacher

group of teachers was sitting in the lovely early
evening sunshine outside the main conference
room of a Christian centre in Green Lake,
Wisconsin, USA. They were chatting idly as
they sat, relaxing and watching the light dancing on the
gentle waters of the lake. One of them, Joe, was telling
the others about some of his experiences in the construc-
tion industry where he had been employed before
becoming a teacher. He had obviously found that work
both interesting and rewarding.

'So why did you leave it all and come into teaching?'
he was asked.

'Well,' he said, 'I've always liked kids, and our church
runs a summer camp for local children, which I used to
help with. Our pastor reckoned I was a natural with
them, and he suggested I should seriously think about
being a teacher. I thought about it for a time, and
eventually decided that God was calling me out of my

job to work with kids. So I trained for teaching and here I am.'

A girl commented, 'That's very interesting. It never occurred to me or my family that I should do anything else but teach. After high school I went to college, trained for teaching, and I've taught elementary school ever since.'

'What about you, Jim?' asked another.

'Aw, I'm a bit like Joe,' Jim answered. 'When I was abroad in the navy I had to do a bit of instructing. I tried to back out, but my commander wouldn't hear of it. I found I liked it, and so, when my period of service was ended, I just went on from there.'

I think it's always interesting to hear how and why people got the jobs they do. Naturally, I'm specially interested in teachers. I suppose most of them entered the profession straight from college or university, like the girl in the group. A few drift into teaching. Some come because they like their subject and want to enthuse others about it. Many love children and teach because of that. Most Christian teachers I've asked, say they felt called or led to teach. In the United Kingdom, for hundreds of years, teaching was regarded as a vocation, a special calling. Some people still regard it like that, although these days you don't often hear teachers in England speaking of their work in that way.

From my own point of view, I believe that most Christians are where they are because God put them there, whether they always know it or not. What is certainly also true is that if God is not happy about where one of His people is, He'll pretty soon take steps to make sure that person knows it and moves to where He wants them to be. The Scriptures are full of examples, and so is every Christian congregation.

Don't you find this reassuring? I do. And I think it's particularly reassuring for teachers, especially when you think what a responsible job teaching is, and when you also remember what the Bible has to say on the subject. The most explicit comment is that in the letter of James where it says:

Not many of you should presume to be teachers, my brothers, because you know that we who teach will be judged more strictly. We all stumble in many ways. If anyone is never at fault in what he says, he is a perfect man, able to keep his whole body in check (James 3:1–2).

Not very encouraging, is it? If you'd never read those verses, you might well have thought that the New Testament would be urging lots of Christians to become teachers so that the good news of Jesus would be spread more effectively. That certainly applies to witnessing. But to be a teacher has special implications which mean that it's not a job for any and every Christian. And when you realize that teachers will be judged more strictly than other Christians, well, that should make us all stop and think before we decide it's right for us to go ahead and take up the office.

A responsible office

Wherever any Christian goes, and whatever he does, he is a representative of Christ, and a witness to His Lordship. But James, as we've noticed, is not keen to encourage too many to take up teaching as a career. Of course, he is thinking principally of teachers of the Christian faith and doctrine. In this context, the word he uses for teacher, *didaskalos*, refers to one who teaches Christian truth in the churches. And that is an office of great responsibility. To proclaim God's Word, and to help others to understand it, is to undertake a commission of the highest importance in the church. Not surprisingly then, it is the teachers in the church who will be judged more strictly than anyone else.

Part of the problem, as James points out, is that we all stumble in many ways. Or as another translation puts it, we all make many mistakes. How does that fact grab you? Can you just shrug your shoulders and carry on? Or does it get to you a lot? I can tell you this. It often alarms young would-be teachers more than it should. I've known many a student-teacher become very down-hearted when they realize they made errors in their classrooms. Fortunately, most of them are not too put off by this. They gradually learn from their mistakes and improve. Even so, anyone who is thinking of the teaching profession as a career needs to face up to this warning by James. We do all of us get things wrong sometimes. So we should not press on to become teachers unless we can come to terms with that fact about ourselves.

You know, I do like James. He doesn't mess about. He writes a pretty blunt letter. And he's so practical. He says to himself: What's the way in which teachers stumble the most? Where are they most likely to make mistakes? The answer's obvious. It's in what we say. And so he tells us. If you're never at fault in what you say, you're perfect and your self-control is 100% right. That puts any Christian in his or her place straight away. Only the Lord Jesus fits that description.

He explained the point in more detail and in a slightly different way. He taught that what comes out of someone, from his heart, is what defiles him (Matthew 15:18–20). Hence the greater need for caution about setting oneself up as a teacher. For the principal means of communication for any teacher is the spoken word. Right communication is central to the task, and the effects of misuse, as James goes on to point out, are extremely serious.

38

We'll look in more detail at all this in a later chapter which deals with the teacher as communicator. The main question I'd like to ask now is this. Have these verses anything to say to the teacher in school as well as to the teacher in the church?

Traditionally, the answer to this has always been 'yes'. That's why teaching has always been regarded as a special calling. As you know, I think that's right. For while the teacher of God's truth in the church has an awesome responsibility to teach rightly, teachers of children and young people in our schools also have a crucial duty to perform. The intellectual, moral and spiritual health and well-being of the young are, to a significant extent, in their hands. People generally have high expectations of teachers, and believe that who teachers are, and what they teach, matter greatly.

So don't take on the job unless you're sure you know what you're like, and what it involves. It's essential that the Christian teacher be wise and understanding, not least about his or her own failings, and the problem of taming the tongue. All this raises the question about the teacher's approach to all he or she does.

Teaching styles: the source

The kind of teacher we are will be revealed by our whole teaching style. And that, says James, is much more a product of what we are than of what we know. Every teaching style has a source. Knowledge has something to do with it. So has personality. So have techniques of teaching. But the source goes deeper than any of these. James, I believe, sums it up in one word – wisdom. So where does your wisdom come from?

Maybe you've heard the old rhyme which children used to chant: 'Early to bed, early to rise, makes a man healthy, wealthy and wise.' Well, there's one answer for you – careful personal habits. I once tried this out on a group of teenagers in a moral education session. They threw it out with scorn, as a recipe for complete dullness. One of them recast it to make the point. He said it should be: 'Early to rise, early to bed, makes a man healthy, wealthy – and dead.' Anyway, teaching is quite an exhausting business, and I do not know any wealthy teachers. So let's ask once again: Where does your wisdom come from?

Lots of teachers say it comes from their studies. They worked really hard when at college and university to understand as much as they could about their chosen area of knowledge. They wanted to understand in depth as well as in quantity. For the deeper their understanding and the wider their knowledge, the better they believed their teaching would be. This all sounds reasonable, don't you think? But a quick examination of the argument shows it to be mistaken. For wisdom is more concerned with the application of knowledge than with the amount of knowledge we possess.

I think teachers who equate wisdom with intensive study do so because they are also misled by a false estimate of academic excellence. A lot of other people fall for this one. They look at those who teach in academic institutions, and, because such people are more knowledgeable and more expert in their field of study than others, it is assumed that they are so much wiser as well.

This idea is encouraged in the popular mind by certain radio and television programmes. There's that long-running show on the radio called *Brain of Britain*. Even more popular is the television series called *Mastermind*. In both shows, wide general knowledge, plus rapid recall of information, plus some good fortune in the questions one is asked, ensure success. This success, and the knowledge that contributed to victory, are greatly

40

admired. The respect is deserved. But not if it assumes that the winners must be full of wisdom as well.

How I wish it were true that such knowledge and expertise guaranteed wisdom. But it doesn't. Certainly, being full of knowledge is very useful. It may well contribute to the wisdom of a wise teacher. But great knowledge and wisdom are by no means synonymous. We should all be willing to respect scholarship, and to learn from the scholar, but such learning has its limitations. It is certainly not the spiritual and practical wisdom that James is talking about.

So then, let's go back to the question once more. Where does your wisdom come from?

The other quite common answer from teachers is that it comes from experience. I once got a head teacher to come and talk to my students. They asked him a lot of questions about his school and about teaching. At the end, he summed up the discussion as follows: 'It all boils down to experience,' he said, tapping the side of his nose. 'You've just got to be patient. You may know all there is to know about your subject, but wisdom comes from experience. You don't get it overnight. You'll see. When you've been teaching for ten years or more, you look back over your past and you'll see how true my words are.'

Now this again is a very plausible answer. My students accepted it, and it seems to have a lot going for it. After all, when you've been teaching for a few years, you're hardly likely to be as green as when you first started. All that initial uncertainty and those early awkwardnesses should have long disappeared. You know so much more about children and their needs, and also what's expected of you as a teacher. And if you've taught in more than one school, you're likely to be even more insightful and wise regarding your work. And your practical skills should be much more polished and assured, as well.

Have a look around any school staffroom. There'll be some teachers of long standing there. They may well be very competent and do a good job of work day by day. But wise? No, you probably would not describe all of them like that.

Nevertheless, many teachers try to base their teaching style on either their knowledge of their subject, or their experience of teaching, or both. But James goes deeper than all this. He sees wisdom as closely related to character, in fact to the whole spiritual and moral outlook of a person.

The two kinds of wisdom

James also suggests that there are basically only two kinds of wisdom. One is the genuine thing, and the other a spurious article, 'wisdom' in inverted commas. Both are evident in the teaching profession. Therefore it's a real help to the Christian teacher to be clear about what true wisdom really is, and what it involves. It's worth listening to James on the subject.

The wisdom of this world

Let's look at the phoney kind first. This 'wisdom', says James, does not come down from heaven but is earthly, unspiritual, of the devil (James 3:15). What do these words actually mean? Well, 'earthly' simply means 'of, or belonging to, the earth', the opposite of heavenly. This 'wisdom' is thoroughly grounded in this world. 'Unspiritual' – it's translated 'sensual' in the Authorized Version, and could be translated 'natural' – relates more to the human mind. It would be a wisdom which springs from, or which accords with, the corrupt desires and affections of the natural man, the opposite of that spiritual discernment. 'Devilish' literally means 'proceeding from demons', and reminds us that some 'wisdom' has its origin with the powers of darkness.

So this kind of wisdom is untouched by anything holy or Christian. It is based on this world's values and considerations, and is determined by the selfish covetousness and cravings of the flesh. It is a driving force which seeks to secure personal advantage and satisfaction before all else. Not surprisingly therefore, it will show itself in twisted attitudes and in wrong behaviour.

James stresses certain specific examples. He writes of bitter envy and selfish ambition which are harboured in the heart. The teaching profession, like every other walk of life, has its share of them.

Attitudes to others show the jealousy which desires to possess what others have or to deprive others of what they have, be it possessions, qualities or reputation. Such envy is bitter, says James. Have you ever pricked your finger with a needle or pin, or cut your hand with the sharp point of a knife? Or have you ever tasted a particularly sour lemon, or quinine, or even the juice of the aloe plant – something with a really biting, harsh taste that makes you shudder? If you have, you have a good idea of what James means by 'bitter'. Likewise the 'selfish ambition' to which he refers has the idea of quarrelling and contentiousness, the sort of strife which fights hard to get its own way, and to promote itself at the expense of others.

The inevitable outcome of such 'wisdom' is disorder. It produces tumult and disquiet and restlessness all round. Worse still, it creates instability. That is the literal meaning of the word, and it relates to revolution and anarchy. Envy and selfish ambition also produce 'every evil practice'. The word here used for 'evil' is *phaulos*. This principally refers to what is trivial or slight, and goes on to mean 'paltry', 'bad' in the sense of being worthless, even 'contemptible'.

So how might all this apply to teachers? Well, I think

it's like this. If a teacher's teaching style is founded on the wisdom of this world, then one thing is for sure. It lacks true spiritual discernment and character. I do not mean to imply that all such teachers are characterized by bitter envy and selfish ambition, or that they boast about such things and go out of their way to deny the truth (verse 14). Nevertheless the dangers of jealousy and self-seeking are very real, and they can easily produce confusion, bad and trivial practices, and the suppression of what is good and true. A teaching style that is based on earthly, natural standards can, by those standards, be very successful. But it will always be limited, blinkered and open to all the dangers of self-direction.

Heavenly wisdom

James tells us that 'the wisdom that comes from heaven is first of all pure; then peace-loving, considerate, submissive, full of mercy and good fruit, impartial and sincere' (3:17). That's eight special qualities. Or if you prefer it, heavenly wisdom reveals itself in eight particular ways. Let's do a quick study of each of them in turn. As we do, why don't you stop after each one and ask yourself how very appropriately they relate to the – to your – teaching situation. It might even be helpful for you to jot down your ideas so that you can share them later with your Christian friends.

1. **Pure** (*hagnos*). This literally means 'chaste' or 'pure'. The word comes from the same root as *hagios* – holy, undefiled, not contaminated – and implies nearness to God. Some scholars have pointed out that the word originally meant 'ready for worship'. So the wisdom from above is clean, unsullied, without blemish.

2. **Peace-loving** (*eirēnikos*). This means 'peaceable',

'not belligerent or aggressive'. Hence the chief concern of this aspect of wisdom is to promote harmony and good relationships, and to encourage reconciliation between antagonists. No wonder verse 18 comments that 'Peace-makers who sow in peace raise a harvest of righteousness.' And righteousness can be summed up as whatever conforms to the revealed will of God.

3. Considerate (epieikēs). This literally means 'yielding' or 'pliant' and so is also translated as 'gentle'. Such wisdom takes full account of others and is consequently forbearing and moderate, not wishing to insist on the letter of the law to promote personal advantage. The notion of being fair and equitable, and of judging impartially, is also present, qualities which children especially want to see in their teachers.

4. Submissive (eupeithēs). Other versions translate this word as 'easy to be entreated' or 'open to reason', and these more accurately convey the meaning of the term. 'Easily persuaded' and 'compliant' would also serve, not in the sense of lacking backbone or weakness of will, but rather meaning sympathetic and prepared to listen without having to be pressurized to do so.

5. Full of mercy (eleos). This word denotes kindness, beneficence and forbearance. It shows itself in active sympathy and compassion, and the emphasis of the term is upon action rather than a state or feeling. So the wise teacher will not simply be patient, forbearing and understanding, but will show compassion and kindness in all that he or she says and does with the pupils. And let's remember that James says '*full* of mercy'.

6. Full of good fruit (carpoi agathoi). Again the emphasis is on what is done rather than on a particular personal characteristic, although it is obvious that good fruit, good words and deeds, and good results are the visible expression of the inner character of the one producing such results. The heavenly wisdom enables the Christian teacher to achieve good and wholesome actions, and success of the most positive and worthy kind.

7. Impartial (*adiakritos*). This word principally means 'not to be parted' and hence 'impartial' and 'without uncertainty'. It means not judging diversely and indecisively. Hence it emphasizes even more clearly than the word 'compassion' (earlier in the list) the notion of being fair and just in one's judgments and actions.

8. Sincere (*anypokritos*). The literal meaning of this word is 'without hypocrisy or dissimulation'. It is linked to a word used of actors and the stage, hence the idea of play-acting and pretence. Wisdom from heaven is not an act. It is genuine, unfeigned, and therefore wholly sincere.

I find it's very helpful for me to concentrate on the details like this. I hope you are helped as well. But then the Bible is like that. It never leaves us with vague generalizations. It always tells us precisely what we need to know. So wisdom from heaven, like earthly 'wisdom', shows itself in two main ways. There's the attitude a person has to himself or herself and there's that person's attitude to others, with actions determined by those attitudes.

A profile summary

What conclusions, then, can we arrive at about the Christian teacher in the light of this passage? Perhaps a final checklist will help.

I have a friend who spends lots of his spare time tinkering with his car. He's for ever taking it to bits, it seems, to clean and test it. I'm just happy so long as my car goes OK, and when it doesn't, I cry for help straight away. Not this chap. He loves internal combustion engines. But whenever he works on his car, he's always careful to follow a set pattern, of the kind garage mechanics have. He's got a special car manual which lays down the order in which things have to be done, and he always uses the checklist it provides, even though he knows so much about the workings of a car.

My wife's a bit like him. She's a great cook, and she loves cookbooks, especially for new ideas. She doesn't need to have the books beside her every time she bakes. I'm sure she could make her apple pies with her eyes closed and they'd still be delicious. But for some things, including things she's often baked before, she still likes the book to be handy, to keep her right.

I know that not everyone is like that. We don't all appreciate checklists. But since the Bible offers us them from time to time, let's summarize the passage from James in that way, to establish a profile for Christian teachers.

Christian teachers, therefore, are:

1. Called by God to the special task of teaching.
2. Pure, peace-loving and genuine.
3. Considerate, open to others, impartial and merciful.
4. Living fruitful lives.

You and I must not be discouraged if we feel that we fall far short of these points. God knows. And by the power of His grace, if He's called you to teach, He will enable you to grow in heavenly wisdom and understanding, so that you can achieve increasing success with all parts of this checklist. As James said, you'll still make mistakes. But the fruits of God's wisdom are still there to be attained, in His strength.

Verse 13 sums it all up. Wise and understanding teachers live a good life in which all their actions are characterized by a basic humility which heavenly wisdom creates in them. It's perhaps worth adding that meekness for the Greeks denoted a strong person's self-discipline and a wise person's humility. To the Jew, a wise person was one who bore himself gently among his fellows. Both views find support in the Scriptures, which, as we've seen, go into much more detail. And success comes through peaceful sowing (verse 18). Paul's example was to warn and teach every person with all wisdom, so that he might present every person 'perfect' or mature in Christ (Colossians 1:28). It's a good model for any teacher to follow.

For prayer and discussion

1. How and why did you become a teacher? Consider how God has led you since that day. Are there any special incidents or moments when you felt His presence guiding you, or interceding on your behalf?

2. Do you think Christian teachers should be different from any other teacher of boys and girls? What's distinctive about those you know personally?

3. Paul is very blunt about teachers who assume a superiority and infallibility based on their greater knowledge and gifts – see Romans 2:17–21. Do his remarks say anything to Christians who teach? Why do you think he is so critical of these attitudes?

4. Consider Colossians 1:9–14, as you spend some time in prayer. What specific areas of wisdom and knowledge would you want God to fill you with, in relation to your teaching life?

5. Let's be honest in evaluating our own lives as teachers. Are we prone to make certain mistakes? How do you react when you find you have been in error? Is your teaching style too much founded on earthly 'wisdom'? Think about this, and perhaps discuss it with a Christian colleague or two. How can we develop a style which is increasingly governed by the wisdom from above?

6. Proverbs has much to say about the practical side of wisdom. Make a list of these practical outworkings of wisdom and consider how they might relate to the situation in your school.

7. Discuss with other teachers the difference between wisdom and knowledge, especially in the light of the Bible's view of these things.

8. Being a Christian teacher inevitably means being involved with children's spiritual and moral growth, as well as their intellectual and social development. Think about how you might get closer to your pupils and help them more positively. Ask God to guide you specifically concerning some particular individual or group.

9. Have a time of prayer and praise in which you bring all your pupils and colleagues before the Lord.

3

The 'three Rs' of Jesus: (1) Receiving and responding

I remember one Saturday, searching the supermarket shelves for the goods I wanted, when I overheard two ladies talking. One had two children, a boy aged about five and a girl coming up to two years old. The ladies had obviously not seen each other for some time, because the one was asking the other about the children. It was impossible for me not to hear the reply to this query. The mother indicated the little girl in her arms, a plump, rosy-cheeked little beauty, and said; 'Our Julie here's a little angel. Good as gold, she is. But as for Peter' (the five-year-old was tugging hard at her skirt, already fed up with standing around) – 'he's a real little devil. Stand still, will you?' she added sharply to him.

You'll have seen incidents like that lots of times. The comments of the mother are familiar too. It's funny how approaches to children vary so widely, even within the same family. Do you have a little angel or a little devil in your home? I guess many teachers think they have such pupils in their classes. And I'm absolutely sure they'll have more little devils than little angels. I know that angels were always in short supply in my classes.

But I have to say at once that teachers and parents who think like that are wrong. Figuratively speaking, there might be just the merest grain of theological truth in the two descriptions, in that children are capable of doing both right and wrong. It's easy to categorize individual children in one particular way. We all tend to do it. But if challenged, we'd have to admit that at best we're exaggerating, and being misleading.

For there *is* an ambivalence in all children. Little Julie may be lovely and obedient and full of charm. Peter may sometimes be a thorough nuisance at home as well as when out shopping. But both are just as capable of the other's behaviour, as biblical teaching about children clearly demonstrates. Every young child, including Peter, has an openness, a guileless simplicity and an appealing desire to please. Each one is also capable of love, worship, trust and praise.

Equally they are naive and immature. They lack both understanding and discernment. And all are tainted with that basic human disease, sin, which most of all wants to put self before everyone and everything else. Hence in every child there are two forces at work at the same time. One would support and promote the wishes and work of their parents and teachers. The other would test, challenge, and even destroy. And just as with everyone else, what they do reveals what their nature is like.

So how should you approach children and young people? I don't know what time of year you'll be reading this, but imagine that the first term of a new school year is looming. You've got your teaching timetable. So you know which class or classes you're responsible for.

You've done some preparations for lessons you intend to teach. And you've had a chat with the head and other members of staff about the new year. Now it's up to you.

The labelling game

First a warning. Remember that mother in the super-market. That means: Beware of labelling children and assuming that the labels accurately sum up individuals or groups. The wife of a friend of mine started a new teaching year with a new class of seven-year-olds. She began, as you would, by trying to get to know them. One boy came right out up to her and announced; 'I'm naughty.' She soon found out that he was, too. But he'd already been branded, with a negative label that he accepted quite readily. And at seven years of age. Oh dear.

No child is ever a little angel or a little devil, either literally or metaphorically. No group of pupils should be described as dummies or flunkies, and condemned implicitly as no-hopers. I've heard teachers describe certain classes as 'the dregs', or 'dropouts', 'bums', and 'freaks'. What an awful way to speak of one's fellow human beings, even if they are extra hard to teach because they are slow learners or difficult to discipline.

I've heard other children described as 'the cream', 'the elite', and 'the tops'. Yes, they may be a pleasure to teach, and easy to get on with, but the labels are equally misleading. Mind you, positive labels are always better than negative ones. When you call a child some-thing, he quickly grows into it. 'I want you to be my special helper,' one of my student teachers once said to a child in his class. Every time this child did something for him, he praised him, using that label. It was not long before he became a real support to his teacher, where before he had been a real nuisance.

But the difficulty with labels is that they set up expectations and reactions which can blind you to other strengths and weaknesses, other talents and needs in your pupils which you really should know about. Labelling may be convenient, but it's often the quickest way to prejudice and the closed mind. And that's a disastrous place to find any teacher, whether a Christian or not.

The Jesus approach

So how should teachers approach their children? For a positive answer, there's no better source to turn to than the Lord Jesus Christ Himself. In Matthew 18, He has some very instructive teaching on the subject.

At that time the disciples came to Jesus and asked, 'Who is the greatest in the kingdom of heaven?'

²He called a little child and had him stand among them. ³And he said: 'I tell you the truth, unless you change and become like little children, you will never enter the kingdom of heaven. ⁴Therefore, whoever humbles himself like this child is the greatest in the kingdom of heaven. ⁵And whoever welcomes a little child like this in my name, welcomes me. ⁶But if anyone causes one of these little ones who believe in me to sin, it would be better for him to have a large millstone hung around his neck and to be drowned in the depths of the sea.

⁷Woe to the world because of the things that cause people to sin! Such things must come, but woe to the man through whom they come! ⁸If your hand or foot causes you to sin, cut it off and throw it away. It is better for you to enter life maimed or crippled than to have two hands or two feet and be thrown into eternal fire. ⁹And if your eye causes you to sin, gouge

*it out and throw it away. It is better for you to enter
life with one eye than to have two eyes and be thrown
into the fire of hell.*

*10See that you do not look down on one of these
little ones. For I tell you that their angels in heaven
always see the face of my Father in heaven.*

*12What do you think? If a man owns a hundred
sheep, and one of them wanders away, will he not
leave the ninety-nine on the hills and go to look for
the one that wandered off? 13And if he finds it, I tell
you the truth, he is happier about that one sheep
than about the ninety-nine that did not wander off.
14In the same way your Father in heaven is not willing
that any of these little ones should be lost' (Matthew
18:1–14).*

Notice first the context in which Jesus sets his
comments about how to approach children, especially
little children. It was a question from the disciples about
status. According to Mark's Gospel, on the way from
Galilee to Capernaum, they'd been arguing about which
of them was the greatest. It was a subject that mattered
a lot to them. On that occasion, Jesus instructed them
that 'if anyone wants to be first, he must be the very
last, and the servant of all' (Mark 9:35). Luke records
a similar, perhaps the same, instance very shortly after
Peter, James and John had witnessed Jesus' transfigur-
ation on the mountain (Luke 9:46–48).

In Matthew's story quoted above, the disciples ask a
specific question about who is the greatest in the
kingdom of heaven. Now that was a question which
frequently exercised the minds of many Jews, especially
the Pharisees and Sadducees. It was a typical question
of the times. Jesus' answer is highly atypical. He does
something which no-one then, and few since, would have
dreamed of doing. He draws attention to a little child.

Not an adolescent, you notice, but a very young child. The Greek word *paidion*, used in verses 2, 3, 4 and 5 of the story, describes a small child of tender age. So it's unlikely that the child Jesus called into the midst of His listeners would be much more than of kindergarten years.

The general attitude to children in those days was that they were of little account until they reached young adulthood. Their upbringing, especially a boy's, was important, but no significance was attached to them as persons in their own right for most of their early years. Therefore what Jesus said about children in this passage would have an unusually startling effect on His hearers, especially as He spoke in the context of status, and status in relation to the kingdom of heaven. That context obviously adds importance to His words and attitude.

If any parent or teacher has any doubts at all about how to regard and treat children, those words from Matthew's Gospel should dispel them immediately. In the eyes of Jesus, the significance of all children is underlined from the beginning by His blunt words to the disciples about themselves. 'I tell you the truth,' He says, reminding them at once who He is and of the authority with which He speaks, 'unless you change and become like little children, you will never enter the kingdom of heaven.'

I reckon that puts a whole new perspective on things. All that talk and argument about who is the greatest looks pretty empty now. But not only are the disciples' attitudes to themselves sharply questioned. These words force us all to look again at children in a more Christ-like way. Indeed, one of the main points that this passage teaches is that unless we have a right attitude to ourselves, we aren't likely to approach our children and young people in the right way.

The emphasis for any Christian is upon humility. The

word used in verse 4, 'whoever humbles himself', is *tapeinoō*, which literally means 'to make low'. The area where I live used to be surrounded by coal mines and pit heaps. Huge hills of waste dug out of the earth were everywhere. If you were to visit us, and a lot of tourists do come to Durham, you would never believe this had been the case. You see, where these pit heaps once stood, there are now grassy plains and open pasture land. The pits have gone, and the hills have been made low. The Bible says we have to make ourselves like those hills. We have to abase ourselves, to be lowly-minded, like children.

Whatever else little children know, they know they are dependent on the adults around them. They have few illusions about themselves. They know that they cannot provide for themselves or run their own lives by themselves. They rely on us for their daily well-being, and trust us to take care of them. They commit themselves to us in simple dependence. It's this open commitment, this willingness to trust, that most clearly marks out those who are able to enter the kingdom of God.

All Christians, but especially those whose lives are involved with children and young people, need this lowly receptiveness of the little child. Those Christian teachers who have no selfish concern for their own status and reputation (even when they are placed in positions of authority), but who are meek and lowly in heart and regard children as Jesus does, are being powerful witnesses for the Lord. For that's the kind of approach to themselves and their students that Christ is advocating here.

I'm sure you'd find it profitable to meditate on this passage and the related ones in the Gospels of Mark and Luke. Among other things, it would help you to spell out in some detail the points which Christ emphasizes most about how to consider and treat the young. It used to be a very common saying of parents and others that children went to school to learn the 'three Rs' – reading, (w)riting, and 'rithmetic. The Lord Jesus also is suggesting three Rs for every adult to take note of. They are the receiving of children, the response to children, and the regard for children. I'd like to look at the first two now, and the third in the following chapter.

The receiving of children

Jesus says that your attitude to children should be one of welcome. The word used here – *dechomai* – literally means to receive by deliberate and ready reception of what is offered. It's used quite frequently in the New Testament, for example to receive a person as a visitor, to give hospitality to someone, to receive a gift, or to respond favourably to teaching or testimony. The stress in this particular instance is on a welcoming reception, the sort of greeting you'd give to friends or guests whom you'd invited to your home.

Just think of the last time you had someone round for a meal or to stay with you. Long before they arrived you started making preparations for their coming. If it was for a meal, you had the menu to prepare and the food to cook, the table to set, the rooms you planned to use to tidy and make warm and inviting. And you made sure that you yourself were attractively dressed and as presentable as possible.

When your guests arrived you greeted them with delight, and handshakes and embraces. You wanted them to feel completely at home and glad they had come. Throughout their stay, you made sure they were comfortable, with all their needs taken care of. And when the time came for them to depart, far from hurrying them away, you showed them how sorry you were that they had to go.

That's how Jesus is telling you how to receive and welcome children.

Just picture them now coming into your classroom on the first day of a new school year. Certainly they don't come empty. They bring their backgrounds, their ideas and assumptions, their needs and problems, their hopes and fears. And the older they are, the more they bring.

Look at them trooping in. Whoever they are, they're still dependent on you. They still expect you to make appropriate provision for them. And they're still capable of trust and commitment to you and to what is good and right.

You are to greet and welcome them just as you would Christ Himself. And in doing so with children, He says, you're actually welcoming the Lord Himself. That's how important children are. As He reminded His disciples on an earlier occasion, 'He who receives you receives me, and he who receives me receives the one who sent me' (Matthew 10:40). It's the same word, and the same kind of reception – a deliberate, ready and delighted one.

I think there's something else to say about this incident of Jesus with the little child. It's this. Have you ever thought what it was like for that child? Just imagine the situation again. Here was this obviously important and impressive teacher. He was surrounded by adults who were clearly listening to Him with great respect. We're not told exactly where the child was – among the group of listeners, or perhaps playing nearby or running past. Anyway, he was close enough for Jesus to take him into the centre of the scene quickly and without much delay.

The child had no idea why this teacher wanted him, or what He intended to do with him. But he went along happily enough. He was perhaps pleased as well as intrigued about what he was wanted for. And then, as he stood beside Jesus, he heard Him say to the listening adults, 'Unless you [adults] change and become like little children [like this child here beside me], you will never enter the kingdom of heaven.' And that wasn't the end of it. He went on to say, 'Whoever humbles himself *like this child* is the greatest in the kingdom of heaven. And whoever welcomes a little child *like this* in my name welcomes me.'

How about that then? He may not have understood exactly what Jesus meant. But he did hear that grown-ups have to become like him to enter heaven's kingdom. What's more, it's people who are lowly and dependent like him who are the greatest in God's kingdom. What a boost to his morale, to his understanding of himself, and to the way he regarded himself. Not only did Jesus help his self-image, but He also received him without any conditions about who he was or where he came from. Why? Because He loved him unconditionally. I guess that child felt really safe, secure and wanted that day. And it's worth repeating that teachers who welcome their students like that are also welcoming the Lord.

Just think about it. When you welcome children and young people into your classroom, you are actually welcoming Christ. As a Christian teacher, you are welcoming them *in Christ's name*. There's a thought to rock you back on your heels. Does it come as a shock to you? It did to me, when I first realized it. And just think of the questions it raises.

Is that really how you receive the boys and girls who flock into your classrooms? Do they know that that's how you are welcoming them? Have you prepared a special menu for them, and arranged the room to good advantage for each of them? Are they truly at home in your teaching areas? Are they glad they've come to your lessons? Are they reluctant to leave when the bell or buzzer goes?

I think I'm blushing as I write all this. When I was a full-time schoolmaster, I did honestly look forward to teaching my classes. I did prepare for all of them. But I did teach some of them more eagerly than others. I didn't welcome every child I taught. In fact, there were some I wished I did not have to teach at all. No wonder some of them were not very interested in the work we did. They were probably not very interested in me either. If I'd thought to welcome them in Christ's name, as He wanted me to receive them, it might have been different. Forgive me, please, Lord.

For have you noticed something about that little child that Jesus called to come and stand among them all? Nowhere does it say that Jesus, before this bit of teaching, had gone out to select a particular child. He did not choose one who was especially appealing, or well dressed, or well cared for, or who was more intelligent or well behaved than the rest.

Not at all. He simply looked up and called out a child who just happened to be nearby. In other words, when he said 'Whoever welcomes a little child *like this* in my name welcomes me', He meant any and every little child. So there's no excuse for you or me or any Christian teacher if we're willing to receive and welcome only certain children, of a particular race, colour, creed, background, ability, appearance and behaviour. Christ's words apply to all children without exception. So your attitude should be an open-hearted taking into yourself of every single one.

I realize that this presents a difficult problem. Most of us, if we're honest, have to confess that such a demand is too hard for us to carry out. Will you let me simply admit this right now, and come back to the point in the next chapter when I'll be examining the later verses of

Matthew 18:1–14? I believe you'll find that it'll be easier to face up to after considering the rest of Christ's teaching in this passage.

Responding to children

Having welcomed your students into your classroom, the next question is: What are you going to do with them while they are there? Here comes the second of Christ's three Rs. How should you *respond* to them? For answer, Jesus issues a warning of the utmost seriousness. Listen to what he says.

> *But if anyone causes one of these little ones who believe in me to sin, it would be better for him to have a large millstone hung around his neck and to be drowned in the depths of the sea (verse 6).*

Both Mark (9:42–48) and Luke (17:1–3) record the same warning. So that underlines its seriousness even more. It's worth repeating that children were not considered important in those days. So this statement of Christ's would come as an even greater shock to them. We don't like to hear it either. How often have you heard a church leader give an exposition on the biblical doctrine of the wrath of God?

It's great to be told about God's love and care for us. But we all tend to shy away from stern utterances like this, and quietly forget them. Yet a sentence like this equally stems from the love of God for his creatures. Children matter so much that *anyone*, not just wicked people, cruel people, corrupt people, but *anyone*, is under condemnation if he or she causes a child to sin. The consequences for such behaviour are fearful.

The word translated 'better' in this verse has the sense of being more expedient or more profitable. So it's to someone's *advantage* to be drowned in the depths of the sea, if such a person caused a little one to sin. Some advantage! And the next three verses stress even further what Christ had already underlined earlier in the Sermon on the Mount (Matthew 5:29–30): that is, the awfulness of sin, and the drastic action that it's better to take in order to avoid sinning again.

You'll recall that in verses 7–9, Christ says it's better to enter life maimed or crippled or with one eye than to be whole and cast into hell. Now the word translated 'better' in these verses is not the same as the word Christ used in verse 6. This time it has a sense of being more honourable, much the best thing to do. So, if your actions (via hand or foot), or if your thoughts (via your eyes) cause you to sin, it'll be much better for you if you render them incapable of leading you astray, even though this means you'd enter life maimed.

You might well ask, 'How does all this apply to the children I teach?' As you look at this question, did you notice how Jesus emphasized their trusting nature? He spoke of 'these little ones who believe in me'. That word translated 'believe' means 'to adhere to, to trust in, to rely on, to place confidence in'. So how do you avoid scandalizing them? That's the modern word which comes from the Greek word translated here as 'causing to sin'. This word *skandalizō*, which derives from the word *skandalon*, an 'offence', means 'to cause to stumble' – by putting a snare or a stumbling-block in the way.

Whenever I think of this word, I'm reminded of a little place in Scotland where my wife and I frequently go on holiday. When we first went there, we wanted to make firm and smooth footpaths around the garden. This involved much digging out of lots of large and small stones before we could lay proper pathways. And some of those stones were real stumbling-blocks, very easy to trip over. The work consisted of two main activities. We had to remove the obstacles. And then we had to lay the smooth flagstones. Then the task was completed, and we now have easy and pleasant access all round.

The same kind of activity is necessary in your approach to children, if you are to avoid causing them to be offended, or stumble. We all of us sin in thought, word and deed, and every teacher needs to work out how to help children to be true and positive in all three areas. I'm not suggesting that you are responsible for everything your pupils think and say and do in school. But you and your colleagues do control most of what they do, and therefore a lot of what they think and say. It all starts with room and lesson preparation. That's where most of the stones have to be unearthed and removed, and the material for smooth paths selected.

I feel very strongly about this. Quite often these days, I hear people telling teachers that they should prepare children for the real world by letting them face up to all aspects of reality, good and bad alike. 'They've got to face up to it sometime, so why not let them see what the world is really like while they're at school?' People who make comments like that are usually thinking of the harsh and corrupt aspects of life. They don't want children to leave school ignorant of what they will probably have to face one day.

I think that's utter rubbish. Especially for younger children. Apart from the fact that most children do have to endure much in life that is hard and often evil, I would without hesitation refuse to teach my students any material of questionable quality or dubious morality. So many teachers seem to accept what the textbooks and other aids offer. The books say that certain material is suitable for eight-year-olds or thirteen-year-olds, or whatever, and so they teach it. The book says so, and so it must be OK.

That's not good enough for me. I'm an English

teacher, and I've seen lots of textbooks which offer, in parts anyway, much third-rate writing, and doubtful topics for discussion and project work. I won't teach that stuff to my classes. I want the best for them, the best they are capable of enjoying and understanding. An essential part of my Christian witness as a full-time schoolmaster and university teacher is to select subject-matter to teach, and activities to do, which are going to help my students to develop in straight and true ways.

So I've always tried to do my best to dig up and throw away all the rough 'stones' I found in my textbooks, and to choose only what is true, noble, right, pure, lovely, excellent and praiseworthy. Those were the things St Paul told the Philippians to think about – to ponder, weigh and concentrate upon. That verse, Philippians 4:8, is a splendid guide for any teacher doing lesson preparation. When in doubt about your material, test it against these criteria.

I know that some people reading this will dismiss the notion as too unrealistic, or as an impossible counsel of perfection. After all, you can't prevent children all through their school lives from coming into contact with what is sham, adulterated, or evil. Indeed, children and young people should face up to these things in order to know them for what they are.

Now as a matter of fact, I don't disagree with this last point. But I contend that the only really sure way to help children rightly to discern what is bad or third-rate is, as far as possible, to surround them with loveliness throughout their early and middle years. When they have some real understanding of right standards, of what is true and good and lovely, they are then genuinely in a position to recognize the bad, the false and the ugly for what they truly are.

So I believe teachers *can* prevent their students from stumbling. They do it by helping them to study and learn subject-matter of good quality, and by teaching in settings that are bright, attractive and positive. As regards classrooms, I'm well aware that some schools are old and drab. But as any good primary school teacher will tell you, it's not difficult, with the children's help, to liven up the place with pictures, wall-charts and creative work done by the students. You can soon produce a setting where sound learning can take place.

As for lesson content, I know it's not always possible to examine beforehand all the material that the children are to be faced with. Radio and television programmes, and some video cassette and tape-slide sequences, are examples.

Children themselves also sometimes bring in tainted ideas. To give just one example, I well recall the horror one of my teacher-training students expressed when she read the stories her class of eight-year-olds had written for her about the circus. More than half the class had concentrated on violent scenes such as the trapeze artists falling to their deaths and the lions mauling their trainer. When she commented on this, they told her that those were the scenes they preferred. They'd seen such things on television and thought they were 'more exciting' than anything else.

Nevertheless it's always possible for all teachers to choose good things for their students to think about and to study. You can make sure that the facts and the skills you teach are the right ones. You can also at all times set before your classes right standards and criteria, and help students to apply them in their work. We'll consider the teacher as communicator in a later chapter. But it's relevant here to add that you can also keep children from stumbling in what they say, as well as in their thoughts and deeds. You can correct their own language and use only good and positive words yourself, in your instructing, explaining, illustrating, questioning, answering and disciplining.

So much then for the first two of the three Rs of Jesus. You receive your students in His name. You respond to them in His name. In the next chapter, we'll examine that third R – regarding children.

For prayer and discussion

1. Think about the classes you are teaching at present. Take each group in turn, and during the next few weeks, pray for every child in the group. Ask God to enable you to approach them as He would.

2. Re-read Matthew 18:1–14. In the light of those verses, how do you receive and respond to your students? What changes ought you to make in your approach to particular individuals and groups?

3. Examine the subject-matter you teach in the light of Philippians 4:8. Apply the tests in turn – is it true? noble? right? pure? lovely? admirable? excellent? praiseworthy? If the material fails any of these tests, discuss with other Christian teachers how to replace it with something better.

4

The 'three Rs' of Jesus: (2) Regarding children

Part of my work is to visit my students when they go into local schools to do some teaching practice. I went into one primary school recently, and sat at the back of the class as is my custom. The child in front of me was quite a problem. He had little self-control, and was constantly standing up, sitting down, and calling out usually wrong or irrelevant answers. All the teachers, as well as my student, had problems with him. The other children were well used to his behaviour, and tolerated it up to a point. However, one of them felt, half way through the lesson, that I deserved an explanation about this boy. She turned round to me and stated with some exasperation, 'Don't take any notice of him, sir. He's just thick.' Ouch.

We've already mentioned in the last chapter the problem of labelling. The girl in that incident was displaying the attitude that Jesus condemned when he said:

*See that you do not look down on one of these little
ones. For I tell you that their angels in heaven always
see the face of my Father in heaven (Matthew 18:10).*

The term He used literally means 'to think down upon
or against anyone'. It therefore implies despising, or, at
the very least, thinking slightingly of someone. He used
the term also in the Sermon on the Mount when,
speaking of serving two masters, He said that one would
love the one and despise the other (Matthew 6:24). Paul
used the same word in Romans 2:4 when he wrote, 'Do
you show contempt for the riches of [God's] kindness?'
and again to Timothy, when he instructs those who have
believing masters 'not to show less respect for them
because they are brothers' (1 Timothy 6:2).

As I noted in the last chapter, Christ's warning was
especially apt for His immediate hearers, since young
children were generally little esteemed at that time.
Clearly, heaven takes a very different view. Their angels
are constantly beholding the face of God Himself, as
they stand in His presence. That seems to me to be a
particularly strong reason why we should respect and
value all children, no matter who they are. It shows how
very special to God every child is.

And yet, as any teacher will confirm, in every school
there are lots of boys and girls who've never been told
this. They've never realized how important they are to
the Creator Himself. No-one has ever encouraged them
to believe that they are special to anyone. On the
contrary, far too many have come to believe themselves
to be useless failures, of no worth or value at all.
Reminders that they are 'common' or 'thick' simply confirm their negative view of themselves. No wonder Jesus
commands us not to despise any child. That order takes
on even greater significance for the Christian teacher.

So how does it apply to *your* teaching situation? How

can *your* approach to children take proper account of the warning? I think the answer to these questions is easy. It's the putting into practice of the answers that's the problem, not least because of the time factor. My reply to these questions is to say that every teacher needs to adopt two strategies. One is to review your perspective. The other is to review your practice. Both involve meditation, and most of us are not so good at that. It takes time, and we're usually too busy. It also takes self-discipline. But if you're willing to 'think on these things', I guarantee you'll help your teaching no end. So why not set aside a little time just before the beginning of each new term to check on your outlook and your activities?

Perspective first. One Christian teacher I know used to despair of ever being able to witness for Christ in school. She was the only Christian on the staff, and felt she was getting nowhere. Suddenly, students started to come to her to ask for personal help with their problems. She asked one or two why they'd come to her, and not to other teachers. They told her that one or two of the Christian pupils had told them about her. It had never occurred to her that they might help. All this led not just to opportunities for her to help students in need, but also to sharing Christian fellowship with the Christian pupils during break times. Her perspective had been broadened. Her 'lonely' position was no longer lonely, and she saw more clearly how God in His mercy works all things well for His people.

Back to the words of Jesus. They remind you to reconsider your pupils from God's point of view. At once you recall the worth and dignity of every individual. They all matter. They're all God's creation. He loves and cherishes every single one. So how could you despise any one of them, knowing that? And then these words of Jesus help you to remember the two main needs that all children share. First there's the need to be loved and respected. Then there's the need to realize and fulfil themselves, those selves that God made and loves.

You'll know the old saying that familiarity breeds contempt. Well, I don't think there are many teachers who actually scorn or disdain their students. But familiarity can easily breed indifference, or a taking for granted, or an impatience. You know that all these are attitudes which many children have to endure from their teachers. You also know that children who are treated like that will rarely succeed at school. They're unlikely to grow up straight and true, with a just and proper image of themselves.

As one boy once wrote in a poem: 'I hate school and everythink about it.' When I asked him why he'd written that, he replied; 'Well, nobody loves you in this place.' His spelling mistake was more appropriate than he realized. For him, at least, every 'think' or attitude was wrong. No wonder he disliked the place so much. What a difference a Christian perspective would have made.

Right perspective leads to proper practice, and that's worth reviewing regularly also. Christian teachers who remember the value of each child will organize their classrooms in ways that don't accept some and reject others. Certain seating plans can do just this. It's very common in primary schools in this part of England for children to be grouped according to their ability in English and mathematics. Consequently, the teacher's evaluation of each child – some considered bright and some thought slow or backward – is obvious to all the other children. The way group activities are organized can also favour some at the expense of others.

Every child should know that the teacher expects everyone to do as well as they are capable of doing – and not some to succeed and some to fail. They should know that each one will be given a real chance to show his or her worth. They should also know that they'll be assessed according to their *actual* gifts and level rather than by a standard which only few can attain. With such knowledge, all of them are more likely to realize that they are loved and that they matter.

Also, let's not overlook the way children are treated. How do you treat your students? Do you praise and encourage all of them, or just the successful? How do you respond to those who fail, or make mistakes? How do you censure the wrongdoers? Do you have favourites? Are you genuinely compassionate, or merely sentimental in attitude? Do you show to *all* your class members the same love, joy, peace, patience, kindness, gentleness, goodness, faithfulness and self-control? Those are the ways of dealing with others which are central to the business of teaching. They also make up the fruit of the Spirit (Galatians 5:22).

So see that you do not look down on any one of these little ones. Keep reviewing your perspective and your practice regularly in the light of that verse from Galatians. If you do, you're unlikely to despise any child, anywhere.

God's attitude

So we have to welcome and accept every child who comes to us. You'll recall that in the last chapter, I confessed that this is one expectation that I find very hard indeed to fulfil. I remember Jack and Peter, to name but two. Jack just used to sit and say nothing, even when he was being spoken to. He never contributed anything to any lesson of mine, and he always did very little work because, he said, he didn't know what to say or to write. Part of the trouble was that his father was wealthy and had the boy's future all mapped out. It had never involved the need for much school learning.

The boy knew that he would enter the family business as soon as his schooldays were over. So he simply switched off in class. I tried every means I could think of to interest and help him, but all to no avail. He just wanted to become a butcher. Even examples from the meat trade didn't really switch him on. Eventually, I used to hope he'd be absent when I taught his class. I failed utterly with him.

As for Peter, he was, when I first encountered him, a tall, well-built, extremely cocky youth who used to sit back, stretch out his legs and sneer throughout my English lessons. Any ex-serviceman knows the attitude as dumb insolence. I found this much harder to deal with than the aggressive or silly behaviour of other adolescents. I could have knocked his head off many times. How delighted I was when he was transferred to a new course and therefore to a group I did not teach. And then I open my Bible and read, 'Whoever welcomes a child like this in my name welcomes me.'

I can't do it, Lord. I try, but I can't do it. I know I ought to, for your sake, and with many of my students, I think I succeed. But isn't it asking too much of mere *me*, to welcome them *all*, and *all* the time? Even the Jacks and the Peters? After all, Lord, as you well know, I'm only human.

Have you ever spoken to the Lord like that? You must have a boy or girl somewhere among your classes of whom you despair. They may not be like my Jack or Peter. They may cause you quite different problems. But they're still a real pain for you. Some teachers find whole classes like that. And yet the Lord says we must welcome every one of them. How on earth can you do that?

Well, I find the answer to that question in this passage from Matthew's Gospel. And I find it, not by concentrating on *my* feelings towards my students, and *my* problems concerning particular individuals, but on *God's* attitude. It's that business of adopting the right perspective again. Let's look at Jack and Peter – you name your own problem children or classes – through God's eyes, as verses 10 to 14 do.

Immediately following His warning not to look down on children, Jesus tells the story of the man who owns a hundred sheep, but has lost one. So off he goes to search for it. What has happened to it? Jesus says it has wandered away. Perhaps it had seen a part of the pasture that looked specially inviting, and had gone to investigate, losing touch with the rest of the flock in doing so. It had been curious, or venturesome, or perhaps wilful, believing it knew what was best for itself. Or it had been tempted away from the others by some means. Whatever the reason, it was gone from the rest, and was in very real danger.

Now isn't it possible to regard Jack and Peter like that? I know that the analogy is not likely to fit every child that you or I find hard to welcome. But in a sense it's true, just as, in a way, the lost sheep partially describes you and me before we became Christians.

Let's go back to the story. What does the man do about the lost sheep? He sets himself the task of finding it and returning it to the fold. This takes a lot of effort. He may have to go to great lengths to find the sheep. What's certain is that the search is highly inconvenient to him personally. He'd much rather stay in the farmhouse, or in the easier, more comfortable pasture with the rest of the flock. But no. Off he goes to look, and he does not rest until he has found it.

I wonder if you noticed that the story is not certain to end in success. I find this especially encouraging. Jesus says '*if* he finds it'. Not '*when* he finds it'. That helps me, not because I might use the fact as an excuse to spend less time over my wandering and difficult students, but because I know that I'm likely to fail with some students, no matter how hard I try. God asks you and me to be faithful, not successful. He never guarantees that we shall win with every child and young person we teach. Even Jesus saw many turn away from Himself and His teaching.

It's important that you really grasp this fact. I know several Christian teachers who cause themselves unnecessary suffering because they blame only themselves when some of their students reject them and refuse to do the work they are set. It's right that you should examine yourself to see if any fault lies in you or your teaching methods. But it's unlikely that you are always to blame whenever one of your students turns away from school, or is a failure there.

The key point of the story in this passage is that the man goes to great trouble to search for the lost sheep. Applying this to your teaching situation, God's attitude – the one He wants *you* to adopt – is to care enough for the stray to go and look, even at considerable personal cost. You may well not win with every child who is 'lost' to you. But you must make every effort to do so, for the child's sake, and for the Lord's sake also.

If you do succeed, the reward is tremendous. The man was 'happier about that one sheep than about the ninety-nine that did not wander off'. Isn't that exactly your experience with a child with whom, after much difficulty and perseverance, you've had success? Let's be honest. Most boys and girls are frankly very easy to teach. They don't present any real problem. But when you make real headway with a problem student, or one with special difficulties, how much more satisfying and heartening it is. Remember that five-year-old who wouldn't come near you for weeks, but who finally trusted you enough to commit himself to you? Or that teenager who, after months of struggling, suddenly realized how to do those maths problems you were teaching? And what about the physically handicapped child whom you finally persuaded to take part in a team game with the rest of the class? Didn't those successes give you a lasting glow of delight? And doesn't that fact make the incentive to search for the straying student all the greater?

But it's the final comment of Jesus on the story that should provide the greatest spur to any Christian teacher. He said, 'In the same way your Father in heaven is not willing that any of these little ones should be lost.' Not one of them. He does not wish any of them 'to be loosed, to perish, to be destroyed'. The word used means all these things. Notice the emphasis on the will of God, and also that He is our Father. That relationship is itself a commentary on our relations with our students. If your Father in heaven is unwilling to lose one such child, then you, His own child, knowing your own dependency on God, should also be unwilling to lose any student.

Another slant on Christ's own attitude was shown by Jesus when teaching across the Jordan river in Judea. Mark and Luke record people bringing their children to Jesus to be blessed. But the disciples rebuked them and tried to turn them away. Mark says Jesus was indignant at this. The word used is *aganakteō*, which means 'to grieve, to feel a violent irritation physically', and so 'to be much displeased', 'to be indignant'. It's a strong word for very strong feelings. Jesus commanded, 'Let the little children come to me, and do not hinder them, for the kingdom of God belongs to such as these' (Mark 10:14).

He then made a comment which echoes the one we've already considered in looking at Matthew 18:3. He says:

'I tell you the truth, anyone who will not receive the kingdom of God like a little child will never enter it.' And he took the children in his arms, put his

hands on them and blessed them (Mark 10:15–16).

I can't resist adding one more comment about all this teaching. I don't know about elsewhere, but in the United Kingdom, primary school teachers feel often that they are the least regarded members of their profession. They think they don't have the status of those who teach adolescents. I think that this Bible teaching shows that *their* work is perhaps the most important of all. The emphasis has been on little children. It is surely obvious that every other teacher in secondary school and college and university depends totally on the foundations that are laid in infant and junior schools. I believe that teachers of young children should take great heart from what Jesus says in these passages.

A last comment

Let's now go back to the Lord's challenge that we should in His name welcome every child who comes to us. In one sense, it's still as hard to do this as it was before we asked the question 'How can you do that?' That's because there's always going to be one child or one group to whom you do not relate easily. Even so, if you stop to think prayerfully about such students, remember with praise that they too were created in the image of God, however blurred that image might seem to you. Remember too that if you view them from the perspective that Christ describes in these passages from Matthew and Mark, then with God's help you *will* be able to practise towards them those attributes which make up the fruit of the Spirit.

It's worth repeating the steps to take, because this problem is such a real one for any Christian teacher. For every child you teach:

1. Remember who created them.
2. Remember each one is created in the image of God.
3. Remember how Christ regards them, and praise Him for them.
4. Remember how He wants you to approach them.
5. Remember to pray specifically for His help every time you have to teach them.

I guarantee that with this perspective, you'll face your problem pupils – and all the others you teach – with much more confidence and compassion. Your whole approach to children and young people will be transformed, because it is so regularly refreshed and renewed. So your chances of success with more of them will be much increased. Hallelujah!

For prayer and discussion

1. How *do* you regard your pupils – as a whole, and as individuals? Should you make any changes? Pick any two you teach and analyse your attitude to them, in detail. It'll help to share with other Christian teachers.

2. Read Proverbs 1 – 9. Many of the responsibilities of the young are listed there. How can you help your pupils to understand and fulfil them?

3. God once made a promise to Cyrus, king of Persia. He said, 'I will go before you and will level the mountains; I will break down gates of bronze, and cut through bars of iron' (Isaiah 45:2). Claim that promise:
    a. to enable you to walk more humbly before God,

b. to help you to overcome relationship problems in your classes.

5

The problem of obedience

I once attended a week-long convention of Christian educators in Florida. One of the workshop seminars attracted more attenders than any other. It was so packed out that the organizers had to find a larger room for everyone, and reschedule three other workshops to new times when they could expect people to turn up. And the topic which created so much interest? It was 'teacher burnout.' On the first evening of the convention I'd heard lots of delegates saying that was one session they weren't going to miss. And they didn't. And oh, how they listened. At the end, one lady spoke for everyone: 'Gee, I sure needed that.'

Why did so many teachers and lecturers go to this session? Because the wear-and-tear of being a teacher is greater now in all our schools than it ever was. School-teaching has never been the easiest of callings. In today's unsettled and disruptive times, when morale is low and traditional standards are called into question everywhere, it's harder than ever. And the biggest cause of teacher stress, teacher tiredness, teacher burnout? It's the problem of discipline. Encouraging children and young people in habits of obedience and self-discipline seems to become more difficult every new academic year.

So how do you keep your pupils under control? How do you make them learn? How do you ensure they obey you? And how do you go on doing that successfully week after week, and year after year? Those are the crunch questions now, the ones most teachers and would-be teachers ask most often. And privately worry about. You may well have asked them yourself. What's more, I guess you've come across answers as well. Cast your eye down every educational publisher's list. Or note the topics that figure prominently at teacher conferences. Books and talks on discipline abound. They're everywhere. Books on how to be a good parent, or a successful teacher. New approaches to bringing up children. Discipline can be fun. And so on. Ho, ho, hum, as an old uncle of mine used to say.

These people give mountains of advice. They write with great authority and conviction, whether they actually teach children or not. And it all sounds so plausible and reasonable. If you work it out, despite some individual variations, most of them make the same assumptions about children and their upbringing. Let's have a quick glance at five of the most popular. Then we'll see how they size up to the teaching of the Bible.

1. Children are born basically good. Or at worst, neither good nor bad. It's their environment that warps and limits development.

2. Children need love, rather than correction. It's not easy to know what those who take this line mean by 'love'. But this love promotes true growth,

while correction represses, producing fear, guilt and inhibitions, all of which hinder development.

3. Direction by parents and teachers restricts children's development. This view argues that children need complete freedom to grow and develop in their own way.

4. Adults have no right to instil their own values and beliefs in children. Attempts to persuade children to adopt the views of their parents or teachers are considered as indoctrination and a failure to respect the rights of each individual child. These rights demand that children arrive at their own beliefs in their own way and in their own time.

5. Children need to determine their own behaviour. Once again the argument is that free, autonomous, mature adulthood can be reached only if children and young people are not bound by the will of adults, but are free to make their own decisions about their lives.

By contrast, James Dobson in his popular Christian bestseller *Dare to Discipline* (Tyndale House, 1971), argues that children need to be *taught* self-discipline and responsible behaviour. He, too, wants children to grow up into mature, responsible adults. The difference is that *he* knows children need help in learning self-control, and in learning how to live. And he knows that discipline which is firm, reasonable, consistent and love-centred is the key teacher.

This kind of upbringing received research backing in the 1970s when D. Thomas, V. Grecas, A. Weigart and E. Rooney published their findings in a book titled *Family Socialisation and the Adolescent* (Toronto: D. C. Heath & Co., 1974). They examined various kinds of parental upbringing and found that authoritative parents, those who were high in support and high in control, produced children with the greatest self-esteem and ability to conform. It was also the children from this kind of background who avoided the youth counter-culture groups and who were most sympathetic to religious belief and practice. It's a pity that this research was not much more widely known.

You might be thinking: 'All this sounds fine and it may well work with many children, if only parents would do their job properly. But too many don't. It would never work with X or Y in our school.' Well, let me tell you about Barry Harrison.

I came across Barry in my capacity as a justice of the peace. He was twelve years old at the time, and his parents were being prosecuted because of his persistent truancy from school. All five of the schools he had been to said he was hopeless, and extremely badly behaved. With the help of a local probation officer, he was made to go to school each day but placed in the care of one teacher whose job it was to deal with boys like Barry. After six months with this teacher, Barry began to make some progress with his school work and had become much less disruptive. He was getting more support from home, also, thanks to the help that the probation officer gave voluntarily to his parents. The teacher had a rough time at first but persisted. He believed in the boy and in the power of caring, consistent discipline. As far as I know, things continue to go satisfactorily for Barry.

If you want to know in more detail how to exercise proper discipline with your students, I can't do better than direct you to read Dr Dobson's books. My purpose in this chapter is to look at the nature and advantages of true obedience. But it does help to remember what the Bible says about the nature and needs of children. You'll find a real contrast with those five popular views about children that we looked at earlier.

As it happens, I've written in detail on this subject,

for instance in my book *Which Way to School?* (Lion, 1972). So I'll simply summarize here. Children, according to the Bible, are not born good. They are born tainted by sin which affects all parts of their being. They are naive, lacking discernment, and their understanding is limited. They are easily led, easily swayed. They are therefore very vulnerable. Even so, they are all capable of love and trust, and also of worship and praise. Their principal needs, therefore, are, first, for love and affection, then individual attention, security and protection from evil, discipline and correction, instruction and teaching.

So that puts the background straight. Now it's time to tackle the obedience issue head on. Let's begin with some stories.

Two Bible stories

Two well-known stories, one from the Old Testament, the other from the New Testament, give us the lead we want. Remember Samuel? When only a young lad he awoke one night to hear the Lord calling him. He thought it was the priest Eli, and three times he got up at once and went to Eli's room. Eli eventually realized what was really happening, and gave Samuel precise instructions which, when God called him again, he carried out exactly, and so received God's message (1 Samuel 3:1–18).

What about the story Jesus told of the two brothers (Matthew 21:28–32)? Their father asked each in turn to go and work in the vineyard. The first brother refused, but later changed his mind and went. The second said he'd go, but never did. I'm sure every teacher has met both kids in their classes.

A story from school

Let me tell you one more story, this time of an experience I had once when visiting one of my student teachers on teaching practice. It was a class of twelve-year-olds that she was taking, and they were full of bounce, and not easy to control. My student was finding it hard to organize them to undertake a special activity that she had planned. One or two of the boys were being particularly difficult. Eventually she stopped the lesson, and said, 'Right. I'm having no more of this nonsense. You'll all sit down at your own desks and do some writing. This is what I want you to do. It's important, and when I read what you've written, I'll know if you've understood what I've been teaching you.' She then issued instructions and set the class to write. After a minute or two, the whole class became quiet, and they worked hard until the end of the lesson.

After it ended, and as the children were preparing to leave the room, I asked two of the naughtier boys separately why they'd worked so well and quietly after being so boisterous earlier in the lesson. One said 'Because I like her. She's a good teacher.' The other said, 'Well, it was the right thing to do, wasn't it? And she had told us it was important.'

Thinking about all this later, it occurred to me that the reasons those two boys gave me, fitted perfectly the two stories from the Bible. They did not do as their teacher had instructed them out of unthinking acquiescence. Still less out of resentful submission. Neither of those approaches constitutes true obedience. Genuine obedience is positive. It is an act of the mind and the will, working together. The mind acknowledges that the rule or the instruction is reasonable, right and important, and the will sets itself to carry it out.

One of those lads obeyed because he respected his

teacher and acknowledged her right, her authority, to demand obedience. So did Samuel. He accepted that Eli was in charge of him, and he respected the fact that Eli was the priest. So he did as Eli instructed him.

The other boy obeyed because he knew it was the right and proper thing to do. He also was acknowledging the right of his teacher to direct his behaviour, just like the obedient son in Jesus' story. True, at first the son didn't want to do what his father asked. But after some reflection, he obeyed. He knew that what his father had asked him to do was reasonable and right. And it was his father who was asking, after all.

Conditions for obedience

Have you ever considered what is necessary to make sure that genuine obedience is possible? I think it's worth making a list of essential conditions. There are at least six which are very important. The stories we've looked at have suggested three of them, so I'll mention them first.

1. The one who commands has the right to do so

The Scriptures always stress that we should obey those who are in legitimate authority over us. These include those who rule in society, the governing authorities, and also, for children, their own parents and teachers.

2. Those who command should be worthy of respect and trust

I'm well aware that not everyone in authority can be trusted or respected. But where children are concerned, this condition is crucial. They should be certain that those over them are of proven worth and standards, people of integrity who can be relied upon.

3. Commands, rules and instructions should be reasonable

Remember we're thinking about the essential conditions for genuine obedience. Pupils in school sometimes have to conform to rules which are not reasonable. And some teachers give instructions which are unnecessary or which don't really further the cause of education. Their children will probably still do as they are told, but reluctantly, perhaps sullenly, perhaps even out of fear. Wholehearted obedience is much more likely if the rules and directions set for children are obviously fair and logical, and have real point and purpose.

4. Commands and rules should be understandable

I am much more likely to do what you ask me to do, or to conform to certain requirements, if I personally comprehend what it is that you, or those requirements, want. So will your children. Rules can be reasonable in themselves, but unless your pupils know exactly what they mean, they will not obey properly, if at all. Failure here is very frequently the cause of pupil 'disobedience'.

5. Those commanded should be capable of obeying

Rules and instructions may well be both reasonable and understandable. But they must also be within the competence of those to whom they are given. It's no good telling children and young people to do something that is really beyond their powers. Yet teachers do this sometimes. And they often get mad when their pupils are puzzled and keep asking for more clarification.

6. The boundaries must be clearly defined from the start

This is absolutely essential to good discipline and real obedience. At the start of any relationship, and especially one between teachers and their classes, what is permissible and what is unacceptable should be made perfectly clear. For all children, boundaries are important. They demonstrate that life has structure and order, and that concern for others is vital. There are those who would remove them, on various grounds. They say that boundaries infringe the freedom of the individual. Or that life without them is more democratic. Or that we should be emphasizing pupils' rights rather than their responsibilities. Such approaches undermine the whole God-ordained social structure and the true nature of every individual person.

As Old Testament references to the removal of boundary stones (for example, Deuteronomy 19:14 and Proverbs 23:10–11) seem to imply, far from helping individuals to achieve their rights or to gain greater freedom, what really happens when people set their own boundaries is that freedom and rights get trampled on, and individuals are victimized or abused. Children and adults alike need limits to what they can or cannot do. These limits provide a secure structure to lean against, and a guide, even a challenge, to conduct.

I reckon the scene is now set for us to listen to what the Bible has to tell us about obedience. As always, the Scriptures give us both sides of the picture so we can be in no doubt about its teaching. We are given examples of disobedience and how to deal with it. And we also have teaching about the blessings of true obedience. I want to end this chapter on a really positive note, and so I'm going to start with the negative side.

Perspectives on disobedience

'Disobedience' is briefly defined in my dictionary as 'rebelliousness' and 'rule-breaking'. It's always a deliberate and direct defiance of authority. It's a conscious going my way to satisfy my selfish ends when I know I should be going in a different direction. Who hasn't seen two-year-old Johnny persistently refusing to do what his mother asks – until an irresistible force meets up with his immovable object? Or the recalcitrant teenager flouting the rules in school or the youth club?

The Bible also gives us some instructive examples. Adam and Eve are the obvious first choice. Do you recall how each of them reacted when God challenged them in the garden? Adam said, 'The woman you put here with me – she gave me some fruit from the tree, and I ate it.' Eve said, 'The serpent deceived me and I ate' (Genesis 3:12–13).

What about Cain? He said, 'I don't know [where Abel is]. Am I my brother's keeper?' (Genesis 4:9).

Then there was Saul, the first king of Israel, when Samuel asked why all the sheep and cattle were not destroyed after the victory over the Amalekites, as God had commanded. Saul said, 'The soldiers brought them from the Amalekites; they spared the best of the sheep and the cattle to sacrifice to the Lord your God, but we totally destroyed the rest' (1 Samuel 15:15).

One more example would be Gehazi, Elisha's servant who secretly obtained from Naaman the gifts of silver and clothing which Elisha had refused after Naaman had been healed of leprosy. When Elisha asked him where he had been, Gehazi replied: 'Your servant didn't go anywhere' (2 Kings 5:25).

Both obedience and disobedience bear their own special fruit. From these examples and others, certain patterns of behaviour can be seen which are born of disobedience. They occur again and again. You'll recognize them in your classrooms as well as elsewhere. Let's pick out some of them.

There is the cover-up, to excuse oneself. So we blame others, as Adam and Eve both did. Or we blame circumstances. It wasn't really our fault.

There is the sullen defensiveness, which Cain demonstrated, when we are confronted with the truth.

There is the rationalization of our disobedient actions, as seen in Saul's attempt to present what he had done in the best possible light.

There is open resistance to accountability, as shown by Adam, Eve, Cain and Saul, a deliberate refusal to acknowledge our sin and guilt.

There is calculated lying, as Cain and Gehazi attempted, to avoid the truth and its consequences.

All such fruit is rotten and must be quickly and efficiently disposed of. One absolutely crucial way to encourage obedience is to deal effectively with disobedience. Read again the way God dealt with Adam and Eve (Genesis 3), and how Samuel faced up to Saul (1 Samuel 15).

In each case, very clear commands set the boundaries of behaviour. When the disobedience had taken place, the wrongdoers were confronted with the facts, and a hearing insisted upon. They were reminded of the commands they had been given. They were asked specifically why they had disobeyed. All excuses were cut through and the wrongdoers made to return to the underlying principles behind the commands. Samuel, for instance, exposed Saul's disobedience for what it really was – rebellion. And rebellion 'is like the sin of divination, and arrogance like the evil of idolatry' (1 Samuel 15:23). Lastly, the penalties for disobedience were very clearly declared.

The blessings of obedience

'Blessed are they whose ways are blameless, who walk according to the law of the Lord.' So proclaimed the psalmist (Psalm 119:1). Even so, obedience for the Christian can sometimes be costly. At our church housegroup recently, we listened to a languages student who had just returned from Leningrad. She met several Christians during her stay, and she told us some very sad stories of how Christians in the Soviet Union are persecuted for their obedience to Christ. Much nearer home, I know of a boy who, because of his Christian faith, refused to join some of his schoolmates in bullying and extorting money from younger students. He was shunned by fellow pupils and also physically assaulted more than once.

Obedience has painful consequences sometimes. Did not the Lord Jesus find that out? He suffered more than anyone else who has ever lived.

Nevertheless, obedience does bring lasting rewards. The Scriptures emphasize a number of them. For example, did you know that the obedient person is much more likely to save on doctor's and hospital bills than the one who disobeys? Surprised? You really shouldn't be, you know. Listen to Proverbs 3:3:

> *Do not be wise in your own eyes;*
> *fear the Lord and shun evil.*
> *This will bring health to your body*
> *and nourishment to your bones.*

Obedience is good medicine. If you think about it, the one who disobeys sets up tensions in himself and others. All those negative results we looked at a page or two earlier inevitably harm body, mind and spirit. And this usually leads to health problems eventually. By contrast, the obedient person is much more assured and at peace with himself and his neighbour. The effect on his personality, and on mind and body alike, is bound to be positive and wholesome.

We ought to remind ourselves of what the words used in the Bible for 'obedience' literally mean. The Old Testament verb is *šāma‘*, and the New Testament words are *hypakoē* (noun) and *hypakouō* (verb). Basically they all refer to hearing or listening. The New Testament word is made up of two words joined together – *hypo* ('under') and *akouō* ('to hear') – to hear under. In other words, to listen submissively. Don't be misled by that word 'submissive'. This is positive, willing, ready submission. But the heart of obedience is real, true listening. ('Be still, and know that I am God,' Psalm 46:10.) It's paying full and willing attention in order to act on what you hear. Your pupils from the infant school upwards need to be trained to listen, if they are ever going to learn to obey.

So obedience, in the Bible, involves two things. First listening, and then the willing submission of self – 'Not as I will, but as you will.' And it also involves confidence, trust, belief in the one who commands. The obedient response is an essential part of faith. Obedience is: 'Lord (or teacher), if you say it, I'll do it.'

I think that the best summary of biblical teaching on obedience can be found in the first letter of John. In that letter, you'll find at least seven great blessings that come from obedience. Our children need these blessings as much as we do. And I'm utterly convinced that they need to know what they are. I believe that more detailed teaching about obedience would encourage pupils so much more. After all, the temptations of disobedience seem to hold out the rewards of excitement, fun, self-assertion, freedom. Why not help show up these seeming attractions for what they really are by teaching the solid, genuine and lasting advantages of obedience?

So let's look at each of the seven blessings about which John writes. Taking them in the order in which they come in the letter, we start with *knowledge*.

1. Knowledge

We know that we have come to know him if we obey his commands (1 John 2:3).

In other words, obedience leads to knowledge. Listen to this extract from a teacher's letter to a student suspended from school for persistent disruptive behaviour:

I know you find a lot of the work hard. And you think it's boring. But I think you can do well if you try. What's happened is no help at all to you, David. I'm asking you to trust me. When you come back, let me help you. I can't if you won't trust me. But if you do accept what I say, and listen instead of causing trouble all the time, you'll soon see how you will benefit. You'll learn more and begin to do well. So you'll prove to yourself that you can do it.

How can that disobedient student possibly learn anything, either at home or in school? His teacher has the right approach. But the children who willingly listen to their parents and teachers, and willingly follow their directions, undoubtedly learn. They acquire new facts, ideas, and skills plus the necessary understanding. It's inevitable. Yes, some take longer to learn these things than others. But the obedient child, given time, is sure to develop his ability as far as it will go.

2. Completeness

It's not very difficult to make most boys and girls realize that to obey those who teach and care for them is a sure way to help them to acquire knowledge. It may be harder to explain this next blessing to them. John writes:

But if anyone obeys his word, God's love is truly made complete in him. This is how we know we are in him (1 John 2:5).

The idea of completeness involves being rounded off, finished, made perfect or whole. This is really the end of all education. You want your pupils to grow into mature, discerning, fully developed individuals. So do I. Willing obedience to those who can help them attain this goal is the path they must tread. By going that way, our students are able to take from us all that we are able to give them.

It's an exciting goal to aim at. It is likely that younger children will find it a hard one to understand. But older secondary-school students will certainly be more able to comprehend it. As they add year to year, so their desire to be adult, and to be treated as adult, grows stronger. They know in their hearts that this takes time. But we can help them realize their progress, as they listen and act submissively. And it's only fair and right – and loving – to help them realize that genuine completeness demands loving submission to God as well as to those in authority. In that respect, teachers and students are in the same position. I think it helps students to know that.

3. Character development

Obedience helps us to mature in character, as well as in knowledge and understanding. This view contrasts sharply with the popular current suggestion that to develop properly each person has to do his or her own thing. Or, as Frank Sinatra likes to sing, 'I did it my way.' The Bible's answer to that is to repeat many times that to grow, we have to do not so much our own thing as the right thing in each situation. John puts it this way:

He who does what is right is righteous, just as he [God] is righteous (1 John 3:7).

Do you notice what he *doesn't* say? He does not say, 'He or she who looks good, is good.' That's what the beauty-treatment ads say. And the clothes ads. He doesn't say, 'He or she who has the mostest, is the mostest.' It's our money- and possession-conscious society that suggests this. He doesn't say, 'He or she who wins, or who is the strongest, is the best.' Nor does he quote that popular saying, 'It's a little bit of what you fancy that does you good.'

Yet our children are constantly pressured to believe that only the good-looking, the successful, the powerful, the rich and the self-indulgent make the best people. And don't imagine they're protected from such ideas inside school. Teachers are as guilty of suggesting these ideas as anyone else.

No. John has a different viewpoint. If you want to be just, unprejudiced, a person of integrity, then obedience to what is right is the road to take. Doing right makes you right, he says – like God.

4. Discernment

Those pressures to believe what the advertising people, the media, or society itself, say, raise another problem for all of us, especially our children. It's this. How can I tell whether what they say is correct, or not? After all, the persuasive skills of these people are great. What's more, most folk seem to believe them. The philosophers of this world are everywhere. And Christians know that the devil himself often goes about as an angel of light to try to deceive God's chosen people. So how can any of us know the true from the false, or who to believe?

Once again the answer lies in obedience. This is what John says:

This is how we know who the children of God are and who the children of the devil are: Anyone who does not do what is right is not a child of God; nor is anyone who does not love his brother (1 John 3:10).

We've just seen that 'he who does what is right, is righteous'. No-one born of God will continue to sin, says John, but he who does what is sinful is of the devil, whose work Jesus came to destroy. It is impossible for the true Christian persistently and deliberately to go on sinning, for every Christian has the Holy Spirit dwelling in him. And it is in the power of the Holy Spirit that the Christian does what is right, just as it is the Spirit of God who enables us to discern good from evil. Faithful obedience to the Spirit's leading increases our ability to grow in righteousness and discernment.

Our children urgently need to learn discernment in this day and age. There is so much to lead them astray. Hence their need, in their early years particularly, for wise, faithful parents and teachers. But the obedient child is growing in knowledge, developing a right character, heading towards maturity and completeness. So he is increasingly able to see through, to interpret, to get wise to, to distinguish between, all the different appeals made to him and the things he sees going on around him. And if he knows it, he can apply the scriptural test to people too, himself included. 'By their fruit you will recognise them' (Matthew 7:16).

5. The life and help of God

The four blessings of obedience that we have listed so far are available in some measure to all children and young people, whether they are Christians or not. Every child who obeys parents and teachers will grow in knowledge, in character, in integrity and in discernment. The next three blessings described by John are the special rewards of the Christian child. But I think all our pupils should, in fairness to them, know these things.

John says:

Those who obey [God's] commands live in him, and he in them. And this is how we know that he lives in us: We know it by the Spirit he gave us (1 John 3:24).

What are those commands? 'To believe in the name of his Son, Jesus Christ, and to love one another as he commanded us' (3:23). Faith in Christ and obedience to Him transform the believer. He becomes a new creation. God Himself comes to dwell in him. The obedient Christian life is a life directed by the indwelling presence and power of the Holy Spirit Himself. The Christian child has become the temple of the living God. And if that were not blessing enough, John says:

Dear friends, if our hearts do not condemn us, we have confidence before God and receive from him anything we ask, because we obey his commands and do what pleases him (3:21–22).

So the obedient Christian child has the life and presence of God within him, and also enjoys His help, not least through answered prayer. This is not some theoretical idea. It is the practical, everyday experience of every faithful Christian. Obedience strengthens that experience. To know the life and help of God Himself is a powerful incentive to do, and to continue to do, what He commands.

6. Loving God's children

One of the greatest joys of the Christian life, and of

Christian obedience, is to know and love our fellow Christian believers. Loving God and doing His will enables us to do this. As John puts it:

This is how we know that we love the children of God: by loving God and carrying out his commands (1 John 5:2).

This is a delightful blessing for the obedient child. This love for God's children brings great joy and encouragement through fellowship with them, and enriches the Christian life beyond measure. Sharing, working, praying, praising and worshipping together is a lovely privilege. It is participation in the joy of heaven itself. And in a hard and often lonely and loveless world, this is a lasting privilege.

7. Victory

It's my impression that our children and young people are more aware today than ever before that life is a struggle. Christian children, whatever their background, will quickly learn this fact. For they are engaged on the side of God in mortal combat with the powers of darkness. This battle shows itself most openly in the unrelenting attempts of the standards, values, and the god of this world to undermine, break, and if possible destroy the Christian.

The world is a most subtle and dangerous enemy. But it is doomed to defeat. For as John says:

Everyone born of God overcomes the world. This is the victory that has overcome the world, even our faith. Who is it that overcomes the world? Only he who believes that Jesus is the Son of God (1 John 5:4–5).

In the war in which He has engaged us to fight, victory is already established. God has already won, because Jesus conquered at Calvary. It was on the cross that all sin was crucified, and all the powers of darkness defeated.

So now God offers this victory to us who trust and obey Him. The world may well appear to be a formidable opponent. But John says that *everyone* born of God overcomes the world. The world may try to cause the Christian all kinds of trouble. But faith in God, belief that Jesus is the Son of God, defeats the world every time.

All the pupils you teach who are prepared to trust the Lord Jesus, to ask Him into their hearts, and by the power of His indwelling Spirit to walk obediently by faith, will know this victory over the world. The child who truly trusts, truly obeys. That child always receives the blessing of victory.

The problem of obedience

So is obedience a problem, as the title of my chapter suggests? Yes, it is. For every child. And every teacher. We all have that in us which wants to please and indulge self before all things. Also, children and young people find the pressure of peer-group opinion increasingly hard to resist. To be seen to conform to the wishes of teachers and the school can bring down the scorn, even the rejection, of contemporaries upon those who try to obey.

This is where positive teaching about the blessings of obedience can help all pupils, those who would obey, and those who think it better, cleverer, more adult (or whatever) to disobey. Encourage them to understand, and prove for themselves that obedience leads to knowledge and greater understanding, to completeness, to character development, to discernment, to God's life and help in us, to loving God's children, and to victory.

I believe that, with the Lord's help, you will achieve great things with your pupils if you do.

For prayer and discussion

1. Read Leviticus 26:3–13 and Deuteronomy 28:1–14, and list the rewards for obedience that God promised the people of Israel as they journeyed to the promised land.

2. Meditate on Romans 5:19 and Philippians 2:8. Then look at Hebrews 5:8. The word 'learn' there means 'to learn by use and practice, to acquire the habit of, to be accustomed to.' What does the verse tell you about the Lord Jesus? How might the verse apply to you?

3. Consider again the six conditions for obedience listed in this chapter. With other Christian teachers, discuss how these conditions might apply to the schools and classrooms in which you teach. What might *you* have to do to make them work in *your* situation?

4. Plan a lesson or two on the topic of obedience. How would you try to teach your pupils the seven blessings of obedience which John's first letter enumerates?

5. Spend some time in prayer examining your own obedience to Christ – obedience as a teacher, as a church member, as a parent, and, above all, as a child of the Father.

6

The teacher as communicator

Sir Francis Bacon once wrote a book on the philosophy of science, entitled *Novum Organum*. He sent it to King James I, who is said to have commented, 'Mr Bacon's book is like the peace of God. It passeth all understanding.'

Ouch! Poor Sir Francis. He clearly failed to communicate.

I watched a lady the other evening on a television programme about deaf people. She used sign language frequently. That was fine for the deaf viewers who were watching her. Her 'signing' spoke to them. But it meant nothing to me because I've never been taught the language.

How about your communication skills? Do your students understand you? Do you 'connect' with them? Presumably you do for most of the time, or you'd be getting nowhere as a teacher. But I wonder if you've ever really stopped to analyse the language you use with your classes. What sort of words do you employ when you are instructing? Or asking questions? Or describing something? How about when you are praising, or reprimanding? Do you ever get really mad with them? What sort of words and phrases do you use then?

And what about non-verbal communication? Things like your body posture, gestures and facial expressions, and tone of voice? What messages do they beam out to your boys and girls?

Have you ever listened to a tape-recording of yourself teaching? Better still, have you ever had any of your lessons, or part of a lesson, video-recorded, so you can see as well as hear yourself? It's a really eye-opening experience. Maybe you attended a refresher course on teaching strategies when the instructor used micro-teaching techniques to let you see yourself in action, if only briefly.

Or maybe you've never had an experience like that. Never even heard a tape-recording of yourself teaching. Lots of teachers haven't. I know one teacher who had the rather weird experience of having a large mirror on the back of his classroom wall. He had no idea what it was doing there or why. But every time he used that room he could not help seeing himself as he was teaching. He reckoned it was a very peculiar sensation. But also it became a help. He became aware of some of his mannerisms and the way he moved. So he got some idea at least of how his students saw him all the time. He said it helped him to become a better communicator.

Examining the message

You don't need me or anyone else to tell you that good communication is central to good teaching. You know, for instance, that you have to use language suitable to the age and ability of the students in your classes. What goes for fourteen-year-olds is no use to the reception class.

Let me just ask you again. Do you ever analyse the spoken setting of your lessons? We all use so many words when we teach that it's very difficult to examine the whole context. Usually the most revealing areas are those direct conversations or interchanges teachers have with particular individuals. In their lesson preparation, they may well have thought about how to put across the main topic of the lesson. It's less likely that they gave much time to question-and-answer sessions, or to the language of planned discussion times.

Nor do they stop to think – not often, anyway – about how they should phrase answers. Or how to word reprimands or praisings. There just may not be time for all that. Anyway, so much of it depends on student reactions that can't always be anticipated beforehand.

For example, consider the following typical teacher phrasings. Out of context, they can't be entirely fairly assessed. But what sort of effect might they have on the persons to whom they're directed? And how will the rest of the class who hear them be affected?

- Come on, Dumbo, I can't wait all day for an answer.
- Mary, sit down and be quiet. In my class you speak when you're spoken to.
- Listen, Jackson, you say 'Sir' whenever you speak to me.
- Don't ask any questions now. Just get on with your work. We may find time later for any queries you have.

Much depends on *how* they are said. The first one could be a real put-down or it could be mildly comic and light-hearted. The second could be sharp and irritated, or patient and said quietly. The third is a no-messing, straight from the shoulder instruction which brooks no argument, and the last could be said in a variety of ways.

But however they are said, they communicate several messages. They make the point that the teacher wants to make. But they all indicate things about attitudes and relationships. And they make assumptions about how teachers should approach their pupils. They also convey ideas, unspoken as well as spoken, about behaviour. And every one of them is value-loaded.

Another 'but' concerns the reaction of those who heard these words spoken to them. Did the teachers communicate exactly what they wanted to get across? Were the reactions those which the teachers would expect or approve of? For instance, if that first example was an attempt at humour, did the pupils really think it amusing – even if they smiled? If it was a put-down, how much did the scorn hurt, rather than stir up the pupil to respond?

These are difficult questions. You *can* measure some pupil reactions easily since many children and young people show how they feel fairly openly. But other reactions that they may have, you can never discern. And you'll probably never know.

This is one illustration of where teaching is an act of faith. You have to do what you believe is right and in the best interests of your classes, and then trust that good will come of it all.

And this is where I think scriptural comments about communicating are a real help. There's not the space to examine them all, so let's consider a few of the most pertinent. We'll begin with the letter of James and taming the tongue.

Taming the tongue

We've already looked at James 3 early in the book. He spends the bulk of the chapter on the problem of controlling what we say. He compares the tongue to the bit in a horse's mouth, or a ship's rudder, or the spark that sets the forest ablaze. He reminds us that man can tame all kinds of wild creatures but he cannot tame the tongue. He says it's a restless evil, full of deadly poison. He underlines our inconsistency. We speak in one breath to praise God, and in the next to curse people who have been made in the likeness of God. This should not be.

Inconsistency in what we say is a real problem for children. The last thing they need is an inconsistent teacher. The person who says one thing today and a different thing tomorrow only causes total confusion in the minds of pupils. They never know where they are with such a person. Many teachers do manage to maintain a fairly consistent approach for most of the time. But failure to tame their tongue still results in lapses, and the effect on their classes when this happens is never good.

So all teachers have a real problem. It's something we cannot overcome by ourselves. At least Christian teachers have the power of God to help. They'll not succeed in their own strength. But by the grace of God they can call upon the power of the Holy Spirit to control their minds and words. So their speech can be a real witness in the classroom, and among their fellow teachers.

I find if I want some down-to-earth practical advice, the book of Proverbs is one sure place to get it. That's where I've discovered comments on the subject from three main angles. First of all, we're given some general advice. Then it examines the effects of wholesome speech. Thirdly it lists some of the results of evil and unwholesome language.

> *The tongue of the righteous is choice silver (Proverbs 10:20).*
> *Lips that speak knowledge are a rare jewel (Proverbs 20:15).*
> *A word aptly spoken is like apples of gold in settings of silver (Proverbs 25:11).*

That's a great start, don't you think? Shows what a privilege it is to be a teacher. The one who teaches knowledge, especially knowledge of moral purity, is very precious indeed. Likewise words which are spoken at the appropriate time, or when the circumstances are just right, are both valuable and attractive. All three sentences apply more widely than to teachers, of course, but teachers can take special heart from them.

Paul puts the point in his own inimitable way. He advises:

> *Let your conversation be always full of grace, seasoned with salt, so that you may know how to answer everyone (Colossians 4:6).*

In this context, that lovely word 'grace' – Greek *charis* – means something which gives or causes pleasure. Words of grace would please those who heard or read them, and create approval. So they'd be attractive and wholesome at the same time.

But they must also be seasoned with salt. Salt can be pungent and sharp-tasting. It's used for two main reasons, as any cook will tell you. One is to season the food it's mixed with, so making it palatable and bringing out the flavour. The other is to preserve food, to make it last and stay fresh longer.

So what we say should be attractively phrased and with a piquant flavour to give our words added point. Such conversation is the sort that enables us to answer all who come into contact with us, young and old alike.

Right. That's the general principle established. How do the Scriptures fill it out a bit, with specific examples? One answer is obvious from what's gone before, You've got to:

Put away perversity from your mouth;
keep corrupt talk far from your lips
(Proverbs 4:24).

Such advice is especially pertinent at a time when the general level of conversation among adults and young people alike has deteriorated. Foul language and blasphemies are commonplace in all levels of society. They can also be heard regularly on television and radio programmes. Schools are not protected from such talk. Hence the example of Christian teachers who refuse to speak like that or to allow such language in their presence is a shining light in a darkening world.

Linked to this is the next piece of advice:

A man of knowledge uses words with restraint,
and a man of understanding is even-tempered
(Proverbs 17:27).

Where words are many, sin is not absent,
but he who holds his tongue is wise
(Proverbs 10:19).

In other words, beware of talking too much, because the danger of sinning increases where words are many. Jesus in the Sermon on the Mount made a similar point. He said:

*Simply let your 'Yes' be 'Yes', and your 'No', 'No':
anything beyond this comes from the evil one
(Matthew 5:37).*

I know that He was referring specifically to the
swearing of oaths, where the temptation to over-emph-
asize is always great for most people. Even so, His
advice is relevant to the point here, and it can be applied
to lots of things we say. Promises we make, for instance.
Praisings and warnings to children, too. Therefore
choose your words with care. And there will be times
when it is better and wiser not to speak at all. In any
case,

*The heart of the righteous weighs its answers (Prov-
erbs 15:28).*

That means the person of integrity meditates carefully
before speaking, and so does not make statements or
comments thoughtlessly. Not always easy to do that in
the heat of the classroom moment, is it? It's an art that
requires practice, as is keeping quiet. But be encouraged. Control does come with practice.

Lastly under the heading of general advice, we should
have a look at two verses at the start of Proverbs 5.
They read:

*My son, pay attention to my wisdom,
    listen well to my words of insight,
that you may maintain discretion
    and your lips may preserve knowledge
        (Proverbs 5:1–2).*

I've just suggested that if you practise saying little, or
sometimes even nothing at all, you'll find yourself able
to control your speech more easily. I reckon these words

107

are even better advice. They let us into the secret of improving our use of words. The fact that the advice is directed to a young man does not mean it's not relevant to those who teach the young.

By sitting at the feet of wisdom ourselves, we teachers will be better able to be thoughtful and discreet in what we say and do. And we shall be preserving knowledge when we speak, rather than teaching what is transient and of little value. We shall be filling our minds and hearts with sound learning. So we can draw regularly from such wells in our teaching, to benefit all our pupils.

The effects of good communication

Now for the second angle on communicating – the effects of wholesome speech.

I don't know about you, but I reckon one of the hardest things in life is to be able to work out the consequences of what we say and do. In our family we have our daily newspaper delivered each morning. One of my jobs on Saturdays is to go to the newsagent's to pay for the week's supply, and I usually have a chat with the shop owner. The other Saturday I commented that he was looking a bit down in the mouth, although it was a bright and sunny day.

'Yes,' he said, 'I was enjoying my morning till a customer came in and was really sharp with the lad who delivers her papers. He was a bit late and she came down to see where they were.'

'Did she say anything to you?' I asked.

'No. She just flounced in, demanded her papers from the pile the lad was putting into his sack, and flounced out again. I told the lad not to mind, and to hurry up with his delivery. But that sort of behaviour really puts you off. I'll be all right soon.'

You see what I mean? I'm sure that customer had no idea of the effect she'd had on the newsagent. She wanted to have an effect on the boy, showing her displeasure so that he'd be quicker in future, presumably. But she probably never realized that her words and manner influenced someone else as well. She wouldn't even know for sure what effect she'd had on the boy.

I had a letter this week from a former research student now lecturing in Australia. Among other things he mentioned a colleague of mine who taught him when he was with us in Durham. 'I always quote him', he wrote, 'when I'm talking about counselling. And I make my students use his methods. It's because of people like him that I recommend would-be students to do their higher degrees with you in England.' See? More effects none of us expected or planned. But this time good to know about.

Christians walk by faith and not by sight. That's particularly true of teachers. So just take a long, slow look at what the Bible says are the effects of wise, sound, righteous communication. Most times you'll never be able to measure these effects of your own teaching. So trust the Lord to use what you say for these results.

A general comment first:

The words of the wise are like goads, their collected sayings like firmly embedded nails – given by one Shepherd (Ecclesiastes 12:11).

Did you notice what the preacher says about the words of the wise teacher? Two things. They are like goads, and they're like firmly embedded nails. Now aren't they just the effects you most want your teaching to have? You want what you say to your pupils to spur them on, to encourage and stimulate them. You also want what you say to be remembered, to sink down into their minds for them to hold on to. A goad was a long-handled stick or other instrument with a sharp point on the end.

Farmers used it when ploughing, to urge on their oxen. I can think of a few oxen I taught for whom such an instrument would have been ideal. The nails the Preacher had in mind were made of iron, and were used to secure something really firmly, to a wall for instance.

Wise words, and wise teaching, have those effects. You must believe it. Go on believing it. The Bible says so.

Don't you feel encouraged by all that? Is your spirit singing? Didn't your heart skip a beat with excitement? Well, hang on tight. There's lots more to come. And it's all just great.

I've discovered at least eight more effects which result from wholesome communicating. Here they are.

1. It promotes instruction.

Pleasant words promote instruction (Proverbs 16:21).

A wise man's heart guides his mouth,
and his lips promote instruction (Proverbs 16:23).

A variant reading of the last two words in each quotation is 'make a man (or lips) persuasive'. Either version is attractive. We do want to instruct and to persuade. It's the pleasant and wise words we use that will do both.

2. It nourishes.

The lips of the righteous nourish many
(Proverbs 10:21).

We want to feed our students to sustain them and help them grow. We also want to protect and cherish them as we try to foster their development. Righteous words do all that.

3. It lasts.

Truthful lips endure for ever,
but a lying tongue lasts only a moment
(Proverbs 12:19).

This takes the Preacher's point even further. Honest teaching and speaking endure. It is false speech which has only a temporary influence.

4. It brings healing.

Reckless words pierce like a sword,
but the tongue of the wise brings healing
(Proverbs 12:18).

Pleasant words are a honeycomb,
sweet to the soul and healing to the bones
(Proverbs 16:24).

So often teachers find themselves in situations where they need to comfort, to arbitrate, or to pour oil on troubled waters. Carefully considered and pleasant words soothe and revive. They bring order and harmony into fraught and painful situations. They help to 'restore the soul' of those involved so that staff and pupils alike can resume their activities in a more positive frame of mind. Remember those quarrelling children you adjudicated for? Or that pupil you counselled who was so worked up because he feared he would not master the problem he'd been set, or finish it in time? Or the girl you reassured about her ability after she'd been criticized by other pupils as incompetent? They were all healing words you spoke.

5. It breaks resistance.

A gentle tongue can break a bone (Proverbs 25:15).

A gentle answer turns away wrath (Proverbs 15:1).

The first half of that first quotation refers to patience persuading a ruler. The words remind us that sometimes we are faced with stubborn head teachers, colleagues and pupils. Where strong words forcefully uttered have little effect, or where impatient words pressed with urgency fail, words that are gentle may well succeed. We also get angry sometimes, and we certainly meet with anger in pupils and colleagues. The gentle reply or comment is the one most likely to cool the situation, and bring discussion to a more level-headed dimension.

6. It enables valid responses.

*[Sayings of counsel and knowledge teach you] true
  and reliable words,
  so that you can give sound answers to him who
  sent you (Proverbs 22:21).*

Just as you learn from wise and trustworthy teachers, so your pupils will learn from your wise teaching. In both cases, you and your pupils are enabled to give reliable and genuine responses to those who ask of you.

7. It protects from disaster.

*He who guards his mouth and his tongue
  keeps himself from calamity (Proverbs 21:23).*

So as well as blessing your pupils, keeping a watch over what you say can also protect you from disasters, and various forms of trouble, which unguarded lips bring on themselves. Who has not come across the teacher who threatened to punish more severely than he really intended? When I read this verse I always think of a former colleague who reacted very angrily to a decision of his head teacher, even to the point of resigning his position, only to discover, after his resignation had been accepted, that he had really misunderstood what his head had said. Things were not as bad as he had believed.

8. It brings life.

> *The mouth of the righteous is a fountain of life*
> *(Proverbs 10:11).*

Not only do you teach your pupils to live uprightly, but when your conversation is full of wisdom and moral integrity, you are providing refreshment for life itself.

I know that your pupils – some of them anyway – may not appear to be listening to you, or learning from your teaching. Nevertheless, *you* can never fully tell. Please allow me to share this story with you.

We organized an evening for parents at a school where I was on the staff. During the evening, one couple came up to me to chat.

'Are you Mr May?' asked the man, looking rather fierce.

Somewhat reluctantly because of the look on his face, I confessed that I was.

'You taught my son for two years and he never did very well with his English.'

When he told me the boy's name, I was not surprised. I'd been delighted to see the back of that lad, because he'd always been a nuisance, and never worked hard for me. So I feared what was coming next.

'We want to thank you for what you did for him,' the man said. 'I know he didn't do well for you, but he

113

always liked you. He says you could be trusted and you always kept him right.'

If I'd not heard that for myself, I doubt if I'd ever have believed it.

As I said, *you* can never tell. So continue to teach faithfully the best things you know, and when you get tired or down-hearted, remember what the Bible says are the effects of such teaching. Not only will your words be a fountain of life for your students. They will refresh and invigorate you too.

Beware of bad speaking

We now come to the third angle from which the Bible views communicating. Peter writes:

> *Whoever would love life*
> *and see good days*
> *must keep his tongue from evil*
> *and his lips from deceitful speech (1 Peter 3:10).*

So as I heard a mother say to her child in a shop only this lunchtime, 'Watch your mouth.' Evil, deceitful and misleading speech will not help you to enjoy good days. Your life will be full of problems.

This time I've pulled out six verses from the book of Proverbs to remind you of six bad effects of wrong and careless communication.

1. It leads to sin.

> *Where words are many, sin is not absent,*
> *but he who holds his tongue is wise*
> *(Proverbs 10:19).*

We've met up with this verse already. I include it again here because one of the temptations most common

114

to teachers is to talk too much. We tend to feel that because we *are* the teachers, we should have not only the last word, but also the first and middle ones as well. The more you say, the greater the danger of erring. So don't overdo what you speak in any situation. To be blunt, if you don't strike oil in the first few minutes, stop boring. Also, the more you say, particularly in a disciplining situation, the more likely you are to say something you may regret.

2. *It stirs up anger*.

A harsh word stirs up anger (Proverbs 15:1).

It's so easy for any teacher to say harsh things to one's pupils. They can be lazy, insolent, slow, perverse, stupid – you name it, children and adolescents can be it. You need the patience of Job all the time. But you're not Job, are you? So you crack, now and then. Don't get me wrong. I'm all for giving a class or an individual a good telling off if that's what is deserved. But harsh words, says the Bible, stir up anger. And human anger is usually sinful.

The word translated 'harsh' – or 'grievous' in the King James Version – might mislead you. When I hear the word, I automatically imagine something rasping, like a file on metal, or a strident noise as in a bad gear change when driving. But the term literally means 'a word that hurts'. Sadly I confess to you that I am capable of wanting to say such words sometimes. May the Lord prevent me from ever doing so to anybody, and especially to children and young people.

I recall being irritated once with a nine-year-old who just wouldn't stop interfering with his neighbours and distracting them from their work. In a fit of anger, I grabbed him, forcibly turned him round to face his desk, and told him sharply not to be such a nuisance. I was shocked to see how angry he became. I'm sure he thought I'd over-reacted. Anyway, he shook with emotion and really glared at me. He didn't bother his classmates again, but he took a long time to concentrate on his work. Black mark for the teacher. I should have dealt with him much more calmly. I had to make it up with him later, but it wasn't easy. He was slow to come round. But that was my fault.

So beware of the harsh word, the grievous word, and most of all the word that hurts. They do harm, not good, even when they appear to have achieved their goal. For they cause others to lose control. And that's a real setback to their growth to maturity and wholeness.

3. It pierces the spirit.

Reckless words pierce like a sword (Proverbs 12:18).

It's not hard to find yourself in a situation in school where you are led to say something rash. You over-react, as I did with that nine-year-old. Something inside you makes you go too far in what you say. So your words are like sword thrusts. They really wound. And the hurt can last a long time. Pupils don't easily forget. No-one does, when hurt like that. Doesn't the very thought of it make you long for the wisdom and meek-ness of the Lord?

4. It crushes the spirit.

The tongue that brings healing is a tree of life,
but a deceitful tongue crushes the spirit   •
(Proverbs 15:4).

I find that a surprising comment. I didn't expect it. If

116

it had said that a deceitful tongue caused confusion, or was upsetting, yes, I can see that easily enough. If you're dealing with lies, or one who tries to mislead you in some way, you don't know where you are or what to do. And you can soon be led into error yourself if you believe such words.

But this scripture shows that the effect of deception, which includes trickery, misrepresentation, falsehood and delusion, is that total bewilderment which finally overwhelms the spirit. You must strive to be open and honest, therefore, in all you say. Children and young people are so easily cast down. Their spirit can so readily be broken.

5. It brings ruin.

He who guards his lips guards his life,
*   but he who speaks rashly will come to ruin*
*   (Proverbs 13:3).*

So the rash and reckless speaker doesn't just pierce his hearers. He brings his own fate into the balance. He's heading for his own downfall. So beware.

6. It has no future.

A lying tongue lasts only a moment (Proverbs 12:19).

We're all tempted to tell lies. We all yield to that temptation, alas. But the liar has no future. The person who is deceptive and who misleads is both planting in and building on sand. His teaching will not last. Neither will he. He brings about his own ruin. The Christian command is unequivocal. We are to speak the truth in love (Ephesians 4:15). Nothing else will do.

Non-verbal communication

Way back near the start of this chapter, I reminded you that we don't communicate just by what we say. The way we say it, and the way we look when we say it, also beam out messages. Sometimes what we *don't* say, as we speak, says more than the actual words we are using.

I'll never forget one of my teachers who, when I was thirteen, caught some of us singing and deliberately making a great noise in our classroom one break-time. Now we were supposed to be a model class – the 'goodies'. We quite enjoyed thinking about ourselves like that. Then Miss Jackson came into the room. We didn't see her at first. She waited until we did. We were shocked into silence. All she said was, 'Is this the best way to spend your free time?' She wasn't mad at us. No lecture. No shouting. Just that one sentence. But I've never forgotten the look of disappointment and sadness on her face, or the shake of her head. That's what really crushed us into shame at our childishness and thoughtlessness.

At other times, the way we look actually contradicts the words we are using. So our listeners get two messages, not one. And guess which one makes the bigger impact. Children love to recount their experiences to their parents and teachers. Can you recall doing that as a child? Did you ever get the feeling that though the adult you spoke to said something like, 'Yes, that's very interesting', it was pretty obvious from the look on his face that he couldn't care less, or had his mind on other things? Teachers, watch out.

I recall going to a dinner party once, in America, where I was introduced to one of the top men in the local university. He was a very able, high-powered academic. He was also extremely sociable. He laughed a great deal, and very loudly. But his eyes did not laugh.

And he kept looking at us, perhaps to see how we were reacting. I respected his intellect, and my host's commendation of him. But I felt sad about him as well.

You see, you speak with your eyes, your face, your body, your gestures, and your voice tone, as well as with your mouth. It's so important that they should always be giving the same consistent messages. Pupils know in a flash if there's any discrepancy.

God's attitude

I think it's necessary regularly to remind myself that just as my pupils expect to learn from me, so I need to learn from the Lord. As a teacher, I have to keep asking myself: What would God want me to say on this subject? What would He want me to do in that situation? We who communicate knowledge, standards and values to others should never forget that in the beginning was the Word – and the Word was God Himself. Solomon didn't forget that. He wrote:

For the Lord gives wisdom,
and from his mouth come knowledge and
understanding (Proverbs 2:6).

And what is the attitude of the Supreme Teacher and Communicator to what we say? Proverbs 6:16 says that there are seven things that the Lord hates. Note the strong language – *hates*. Among them are listed the following:

A lying tongue (Proverbs 6:17).

A false witness who pours out lies
and a man who stirs up dissension among his
brothers (Proverbs 6:19).

Proverbs 12:22 makes the same point, but also stresses what gives God great pleasure:

The Lord detests lying lips,
but he delights in men who are truthful.

You'll not be surprised at any of that. But it's a salutary reminder to all teachers that the Lord detests deceitful and any other kind of evil speech. It's equally encouraging to know of His great pleasure in the truth and those who speak it. Those whose words are always wholesome. I'm sure you've got the message.

In each of the earlier sections, we found a New Testament comment to provide a general summary. Perhaps something the Lord Jesus once said should conclude this chapter for us. It makes solemn reading. He had been criticizing the Pharisees, reminding them (and us) that it is out of the overflow of the heart that the mouth speaks. Hence the good person brings good things out of the good stored up in him, and the evil person brings evil things out of the evil stored up in him. And then Jesus asserted:

But I tell you that men will have to give account on the day of judgment for every careless word they have spoken. For by your words you will be acquitted, and by your words you will be condemned (Matthew 12:36–37).

For prayer and discussion

1. Get hold of a Bible concordance – a good Bible dictionary should help as well – and look up 'Words', 'Speech', 'Mouth'. Compare the teaching of the verses which use these terms with those quoted in this chapter. In what ways do they chal-

lenge and encourage you further?

2. Go back over your time in school last week. Some incidents may stand out in your memory. What exactly did you say then? How does it measure up against the teaching of the Bible?

3. If you can possibly tape-record one of your lessons, do so, and then examine critically all the things you said. If you're brave enough, ask another Christian to sit and listen with you, to give another more objective reaction.

4. On your knees, pray and meditate upon David's prayer:

May the words of my mouth, and the meditation of
    my heart
      be pleasing in your sight,
      O Lord, my rock and my Redeemer (Psalm
      19:14).

7

The teacher as shepherd

In my office at the university, at least once every week there appears on my desk a catalogue from some publishing company advertising their new and forthcoming books in the field of education. There are all the usual things listed – works on child development and sociology, on educational theory and methods of teaching, on curriculum matters and teaching aids, and so on. Nearly always there's a section on guidance and counselling. And frequently, that's the largest section in the catalogue. I shouldn't be at all surprised to discover that in the UK and USA more books are now being published on problems of pastoral care than on any other topic.

I'm sure you know that as far as education is concerned, there are three main areas of counselling theory and practice. They all aim to help pupils during their school days and afterwards. There's vocational guidance, which concentrates on their future in the world of work. Then there's educational guidance, which deals with all matters concerning a pupil's academic progress in school. Lastly, there is personal guidance, which concentrates on a pupil's personal needs and problems.

All the best books on the subject stress the importance of making all three types of counselling available to all pupils during their school lives. Seems reasonable, don't you think? And all the best books also stress that all schools, especially comprehensive schools and sixth-form colleges, should include on their staff at least one trained counsellor.

But this leaves the question: What about all the other teachers? Don't they inevitably have pupils coming to them with personal and educational problems? They wouldn't send every boy and girl to see the school counsellor every time. In any case, not every problem requires the help of a person with such training. And doesn't every teacher also have lots of pupils with personal, educational and vocational problems who don't, and won't, go to see anybody about them? What happens in all these cases? What should each teacher do? In particular, what should the Christian teacher do?

What is pastoral care?

When I first entered the teaching profession, I was told that every teacher was, to some extent, *in loco parentis* to every child. Part of my role was to be a kind of parent to my pupils during the time they were in my charge. The most common phrase used today to describe this side of a teacher's work is 'pastoral care'. I don't know about you, but I don't hear much now about the *in loco parentis* bit. But I do know that all teachers are led to expect to play some pastoral role on behalf of their students. And I suspect that by 'pastoral care' most people mean pretty well what used to be implied by the phrase *in loco parentis*.

I guess what most parents and school governors want the teachers to do is to keep a quietly watchful eye on their children. They want them to help when the children are having difficulties or are in trouble. They want them to encourage good and responsible behaviour. They want them to be friends in need and experts when professional help is required.

The trouble is that parents differ in their expectations. So do the school governors. So do teachers themselves. There's a lot of confusion surrounding this aspect of the teacher's role. So why don't we examine it a little, in the light of Holy Scripture?

According to my dictionary, 'pastoral' relates to shepherds, and has to do with flocks and herds. Matthew once wrote of Jesus like this:

> *When he saw the crowds, he had compassion on them, because they were harassed and helpless, like sheep without a shepherd (Matthew 9:36).*

The Bible often describes people as being like sheep. So if adults are like sheep, how much more will children be in need of shepherds to guide and help them?

But what *exactly* is the job of a shepherd? If we can answer that question, we may well be clearer about what every teacher's pastoral role really involves.

The role of a shepherd

One good way to find out is actually to ask a shepherd about his job. You'll probably not know one yourself. But you can always read a lovely book by Phillip Keller entitled *A Shepherd Looks at Psalm 23* (Pickering & Inglis, 1979). That will give you lots of insight, not only about the work of a shepherd, but also about the nature and problems of sheep. Phillip Keller was a shepherd. So he knows.

But the Bible itself gives us lots of clues, in several places. I think one of the most illuminating is chapter 34 of the prophet Ezekiel. Just consider these verses, for instance:

Should not shepherds take care of the flock? (verse 2).

You have not strengthened the weak or healed the sick or bound up the injured. You have not brought back the strays or searched for the lost (verse 4).

As a shepherd looks after his scattered flock when he is with them, so will I look after my sheep (verse 12).

I will bring them out from the nations and gather them from the countries, and I will bring them into their own land. I will pasture them . . . (verse 13).

I will tend them in a good pasture. . . . they will lie down in good grazing land, and there they will feed in a rich pasture (verse 14).

I myself will tend my sheep and make them lie down, declares the Sovereign Lord (verse 15).

I will shepherd the flock with justice (verse 16).

I will judge between one sheep and another (verse 17).

Must my flock feed on what you have trampled and

drink what you have muddied with your feet? (verse 19).

I myself will judge between the fat sheep and the lean sheep (verse 20).

I will . . . rid the land of wild beasts so that they may live . . . and sleep . . . in safety (verse 25).

The whole chapter is worth reading. You'll see that God is criticizing the shepherds who care for themselves but not the flock. And then He promises to take over the role of shepherd Himself to protect and keep the sheep properly. We can summarize the shepherd's duties from these verses. They are:

- To take care of the flock and look after them.
- To strengthen the weak.
- To heal the sick.
- To bind up the injured.
- To bring back the strays.
- To search for the lost.
- To tend the sheep and make them lie down in a good, rich pasture.
- To shepherd them with justice, judging between the fat and the lean, protecting the weak from the strong.
- To protect the grazing and water supplies.
- To rid the land of wild beasts, to make the land safe for the sheep.

One look at that list and you see immediately that we're into a whole new ball game. I'm not suggesting that those who write about pastoral care in school do not have good and helpful things to say. But these verses from Ezekiel – and there are other biblical statements still to consider – reveal the shepherd's role as much more than that of a guide and counsellor.

From that list we can deduce at least three aspects of that role. These are: protection, provision of good pasturage, and personal attention. The order in which we consider them doesn't really matter since all of them are important. Let's begin with the provision of food.

Food provision

The shepherd has to find good pasturage for his flock. They need good grazing land if they are to flourish. They also need plenty of fresh water nearby. Part of the shepherd's task is also to protect the pasturage from the sheep themselves and from other animals. So he must not allow over-grazing, or the land to be trampled down, and the streams muddied and fouled. God promises for His flock, His people, feeding in a rich pasture. Such land will be free of poisonous weeds and infection from other animals. The grass will be lush and juicy, full of goodness.

How might all this apply to the teacher-shepherd? I think we could fairly say that pastoral care in this case includes a rigorous study of curriculum content, making sure that what pupils are taught is appropriate, properly nourishing, and without harmful influences. So lesson content will suit the age and ability of the children. It will be selected to keep from our classes ideas, illustrations, stories and other subject-matter which might harm, rather than feed their minds positively.

You might well ask, 'By what criteria should we judge what is suitable?' Well, I think that the best academic food we can offer to our children and young people is subject-matter which makes them think about whatever is true, noble, right, pure, lovely, excellent and praise-worthy (Philippians 4:8). If you want a slogan, how about this one? Surround them with loveliness. That way their hearts and minds are likely to develop in a much healthier and more positive way.

Protection

Sheep are very vulnerable creatures. They're also a bit stupid, to say the least. So they're always likely to stray. When you're out in the country, in my part of England at least, you're always likely to find one or two sheep that have managed somehow to get through a gate or hedge. They wander along the roads, browsing on the grass verges, usually with no clue as to how to find their way back to the field where the shepherd left them. Many get knocked down and killed or injured by passing vehicles. In wilder country than mine, there's still the danger of wolves and other wild beasts coming down to attack the flock.

A more common danger is from poisonous weeds or plants. Fields where sheep are to be allowed to graze have to be carefully checked to see that the pasturage is free of such harmful growth. And because, as we said earlier, sheep and other animals can foul the land with infectious droppings or by crushing the grass so that its edible value is much reduced, so the shepherd has to oversee the fields to keep them in good shape for the flock. He has to protect them from their own weaknesses.

Our pupils also all need this kind of protection. Most important of all is protection from falsehood. There are many false teachers around. Like many school text-books, they wittingly and unwittingly purvey false ideas, attitudes and values. For example, one of the most common notions abroad today in many subject areas is the suggestion that all values are relative. As a Christian you know this is just not true. There *is* revealed, objective truth, and every Christian is a guardian of this revelation. Anything opposed to this truth is plain error and it needs to be exposed as such.

And it's not indoctrination to make your pupils aware of these facts. On the contrary, it's your duty. All this means that you must be really alert. You can't afford to relax your vigilance for a moment. You need to have carefully considered what your pupils are going to read, and watch, and listen to, before they come across it in the classroom, in your lessons.

Of course they'll come across false and perverted, coarse and cruel, violent and prurient ideas and stories outside your classroom. They'll bring some of these things inside from time to time. That's where you'll need to protect some pupils from their fellows, and to protect those who bring in such information and attitudes from themselves, if necessary.

One teacher I know caught one of his thirteen-year-old boys reading a pornographic magazine. He immediately confiscated this, and, since the class knew what was happening, he used the opportunity to talk about the dangers of such warped and dehumanized material. But the matter did not end there. He wrote a letter to the parents, enclosing the magazine. He pointed out that *he* could control only what his pupils read in class. This he would continue to do. But it was the parents' job to oversee what their children read elsewhere.

When I first heard this story, others present reacted with mixed feelings. One said this was telling tales and the teacher should not have done this. But the teacher concerned replied that the boy had claimed that his parents did not object to his reading the magazine. And in any case, the ultimate responsibility was the parents'. Perhaps they needed to be reminded of this. Most of those listening agreed with this last point. One commented that the suggestion of tale-telling was misleading. Teachers have some responsibility for the spiritual and mental health of their pupils. This teacher had put the boy's best interests first by doing what he did.

Next, the weaker pupils need to be protected from the stronger. This doesn't just mean preventing bullying and cruelty inflicted by older and stronger pupils on the younger and more timid. I believe it means preventing some pupils feeling inferior, because they're not as good academically or in sport or drama or music as the rest of their class. It's up to Christian teachers to try to protect all their pupils.

Lastly, some children need to be protected from themselves. The young are easily led, as you know – by their own desires as well as by the ideas and example of others. For example, some teachers of fourteen- and fifteen-year-olds will have met the problem of the use of contraceptives by children under the age of sixteen.

Mandy actually went to see her teacher about it. She wanted the teacher to support her in asking her doctor for that kind of help. When the teacher counselled her to wait and talk to her parents first, Mandy reacted in the usual way. 'It's my body to do what I like with. I'm old enough to be responsible for myself. Everyone else is doing it, so why shouldn't I? And anyway, my parents wouldn't understand.' And so on. All her teacher was then able to do was to warn her about the long-term consequences, and they also had a helpful discussion about the true nature of love. I don't know what happened with Mandy, except that she went away much more thoughtfully and quietly.

Peter and Karen presented their teachers with an even more difficult problem. They were both convinced that they were 'useless', 'no good to anyone'. Their view of themselves was just one great low. To help them see that they were each in their own special way unique and worthwhile was a long, long job. But they both urgently needed protecting from their own bitter self-denigration.

Here's just one more example out of many I could share with you. Bob was an able student but he'd started to let his work slide. He wasn't anywhere near fulfilling his potential. He just lazed around and did the minimum of work. One day, in a typing class, he was idling away. His tutor, a Christian, watched him for a time and then walked round the class till he arrived at Bob's desk. 'Move over', he ordered, and sat down beside him. Then he looked at the blank sheet in Bob's typewriter, and typed on it, 'From everyone who has been given much, much will be demanded' (Luke 12:48). 'Think about that', he said, as he stood up. 'You have so much talent. Do you really have to waste it?' Bob remained still for a time, and then began to do the work set. Much later he confessed that it was this 'word from the Lord' that changed his attitude.

With Bob, the teacher's protection and personal challenge worked. It doesn't always appear to do so. But that shouldn't stop you trying. Because just as sheep get lost owing to their stupidity and silliness, so do children and young people. So your protective role will never cease to be important.

Personal attention

When I first joined the staff of Durham University, I had a colleague who had taught primary-school children in North Yorkshire, where sheep-farming is one of the main activities. He'd been in the school only a short time when he decided that a good introduction to one of his lessons would be to ask a few questions about sheep. You can see he was well taught himself. 'Start where the children are.' 'Use the knowledge the class already has.' I guess you too learned maxims like these when you did your teaching training. Anyway, he thought he was on good ground to introduce his lesson in that way.

He began by pinning up a picture of a sheep. 'What's that?' he asked. Dead silence. He couldn't believe it. So

131

he picked on one boy. 'Jimmy, you must know. After all, your Dad's a farmer.' No answer. 'Oh, come on. It's so easy', he pleaded. 'Please sir,' replied the boy very hesitantly, 'I don't know. You see, sir, I can't tell from the picture whether it's a Swaledale or a Southdown. And we have only Wensleydale Longwools on our farm.'

End of the lesson – for the teacher. The answer he wanted and expected was of course 'A sheep'. To him, all sheep were – well, just sheep. His pupils knew better. They knew that there are lots of different varieties. I once asked a shepherd about this, and he reeled off over forty different names as quick as a flash of lightning. And he was mentioning only breeds which he knew about in England.

Children are the same. You may have a class of five- or fifteen-year-olds. But they're all individuals, with individual needs, even though they are at the same stage of their education. I know that's obvious. But it's easy to forget in the busy life a teacher has. It's much easier to treat them all the same when you're teaching them. Don't you do that sometimes? I know I do. But Ezekiel reminds us that we can't do that and still do our job properly.

The shepherd has to recognize and deal with the sheep as their individual wants arise. So the weak need strengthening with extra and richer food – or more personal attention and assistance. Some need healing – special care, or special teaching to help them overcome physical or mental disabilities which hinder their progress. The injured need binding up – whether they fell in the playground, were in a fight, or were hurt by cruel taunts, or the unkindness of others. The strays need bringing back and the lost finding. This could mean hunting out the truants or those in trouble outside school and giving them special counselling help and support. It certainly means being available for those pupils who would never seek help for themselves from the school.

132

Those are the ones you usually have to take the initiative with. This is hard, and you may have to bear lots of rebuffs. But when such a pupil learns to open up a bit, the rewards for both of you can be the best part of being a teacher.

All this, as you very well know, takes time. That's costly in any busy teacher's life. But it's worth giving. Remember the example of Jesus who always gave time for those who needed Him. Something else He always did was to listen to those who came to Him. Getting to know any individual involves listening to him or her. That's never very easy. I agree with John and Paula Sandford, who make this perceptive comment in their book *Restoring the Christian Family* (Bridge Publishing, 1984):

> *Real listening is the most difficult art in the world, precisely because it calls for the most complete and constant death of self (p. 67).*

Are you prepared to die to self in order truly to hear and understand your students? After all, as a Christian, you know that every child is important. They are all God's creation, and therefore of supreme worth and dignity. Yes, all of them.

You know your colleagues don't all think like that about them. You may even be the only one on your school staff who does. Your ready help of individuals may well be one of the most conspicuous parts of your witness for Christ in your school, even though you never try to publicize what you do, and even though you're not in the least conscious of the fact.

The example of Jesus

Ezekiel underlines most of the duties of a responsible

shepherd. But he does not mention them all. Not surprisingly, Jesus has important details to add, in His teaching about Himself as the good Shepherd. Some of His words on the subject are well worth examining with teaching in mind. This is what He says:

The sheep listen to his [the shepherd's] voice. He calls his own sheep by name and leads them out. When he has brought out all his own, he goes on ahead of them, and his sheep follow him because they know his voice. But they will never follow a stranger; in fact, they will run away from him because they do not recognize a stranger's voice (John 10:3–5).

I am the good shepherd. The good shepherd lays down his life for the sheep (John 10:11).

I am the good shepherd; I know my sheep and my sheep know me (John 10:14).

Earlier in the chapter, we listed ten duties of a shepherd, as Ezekiel saw them. Now we can add three more, and a warning. Here they are, in the order suggested by the verses quoted.

- The good shepherd knows every sheep by name, and they know him.
- The good shepherd goes ahead of his sheep, leading them.
- The good shepherd sacrifices himself for his sheep.

And the warning is that the sheep will never follow a stranger.

Let's consider the warning first. Are you a stranger to any of your students? How well do they really know you? My experience is that it's quite possible to teach a class for a year or more, and, as far as a few are concerned, to be somewhat remote and unknown even after all that time. Such a situation is more likely if you see the class only once or twice a week. But if you're a stranger to them, then they will avoid you. They won't open up for you. They'll even run away from you.

On the other hand, I know it's possible to teach a class only once each week, and still for every pupil to know you well. The solution lies in your own hands. If you really make an effort to know all your pupils and to make sure they know you – and I have to do this every year with all my students – then your sheep will listen to your voice and follow you. Because they know you.

You see, we're already into the first of those duties just listed. It's really a reinforcement of the point about personal attention. By stressing the personal knowledge shared between shepherd and sheep, between teacher and pupil, the Bible is underlining the importance of such a close relationship.

Richard Baxter, that great Reformed pastor of the seventeenth century, who did such a marvellous work for the Lord in Kidderminster, made the point like this. He said that the Lord's challenge to every pastor is: 'Were they worth my blood, and are they not worth thy labour? It is thy *honour* to be so employed.'

Jesus reminds us next that the good shepherd collects all his sheep together, brings them out and then goes on ahead of them. To me, this suggests that the teachers have an important leadership role as they perform their pastoral duties.

Now this idea is not popular with some influential writers today. Think of Carl Rogers and all the other advocates of non-directive counselling. Their line is to put the teacher in the background and let the students be totally responsible for their own learning. Such

135

people argue that teachers should be neutral. They should not try to influence their classes in specific directions, because this is to encroach on the students' freedom to develop in their own way.

I think this is total nonsense. Such a view makes assumptions about human nature and human ability which are contrary to biblical teaching about our creaturely dependence. It is an abdication of responsibility to behave like that, and it is a confusion and a let-down for the children. They, primary- and secondary-school pupils alike, expect us to set an example and give them a lead. That's what we're qualified to do. It's what the office of teacher demands of us.

And in saying this, I'm not at all implying that our teaching should be totally directive. Of course you want your pupils to discover things for themselves. Of course you want them to learn to make their own minds up and to recognize their own personal responsibility for their views and actions. In no way am I advocating indoctrination or the subjection of pupils. That would apply only if teachers prevented their pupils from considering various viewpoints (in lessons where these are relevant), and demanded of them total, unquestioning docility.

Good shepherd-teachers know the best ways forward for their classes. So they set an example and lead from the front. That still leaves masses of opportunities for the students to question, to undertake personal study and research, and to develop their own talents. But they expect their teachers to know what is needful for them and to provide it in ways they can comprehend.

Lastly, the good shepherd lays down his life for his sheep. This underlines the sacrificial nature of pastoral care. It's very demanding. It does so often require a denial of self to put the pupils first. Every teacher has the need, as well as the right, for time off for personal refreshment. Christian teachers should not forget that.

In your zeal to serve others, you can wear yourself out. Then you'll be of little use to anyone, yourself included. But if you really want to be the kind of teacher Jesus was, then there'll be lots of times when you have to put the Lord's will and your pupils first, rather than yourself.

Pastoring yourself

So being a kind of pastor to your students is a much more demanding job than appears at first sight. I think what the Bible has been saying is relevant to every teacher, not just the school guidance experts. Those special counsellors may still be necessary. But their job is made more clear-cut if teachers undertake these more general pastoral duties which the Bible lists for us.

And that brings me to a final piece of advice from the Scriptures. It's what Paul said to the elders of the church at Ephesus. Here it is:

> *Keep watch over yourselves and all the flock of which the Holy Spirit has made you overseers (Acts 20:28).*

Paul commands them to be 'shepherds of the church of God', and to beware of savage wolves who will come in and not spare the flock (Acts 20:28–29). But did you notice where he started? He said: Keep watch over yourselves.

If you're going to be a good teacher, you do need to keep a close eye on yourself as well as on your pupils. To do that properly, I'm sure, means taking care of yourself. It means not overdoing things. It means not taking on too many responsibilities. (And that might well mean resisting requests for help from your church pastor and others in your church.) It means not wearing yourself out by neglecting your personal life, your diet, and your rest and sleep time. Your personal fitness is important. It's not everything. But it is part of being a good pastor-teacher.

The best teachers are ones in whom there is no dichotomy between what they teach and what they are. You and I need to present ourselves, by the grace of God, as attractive and consistent examples of personal authenticity. We have to be genuine through and through. That way we shall convince as much if not more by what we are than by what we say and teach. Because that way we are free to be used by God for His glory and His purposes.

So as you submit yourself to the Lord Jesus Christ, the great Shepherd of the sheep, your God will equip you with everything good for doing His will in your school and life. May He work in all of us what is pleasing to Him, through Jesus Christ our Lord (*cf.* Hebrews 13:20–21).

For prayer and discussion

1. Read Ezekiel 34 and John 10 once more, and meditate on Christ as the good Shepherd. With the help of a good concordance or Bible dictionary, you could look up other scriptural references to the work of a shepherd and pastor.

2. Consider, with other Christian teachers, how you might seek out and help some of the lost sheep in your school.

3. Have a time of prayer for all who teach, committing their pastoral duties to God.

4. Re-read Psalm 23. In what ways does it add to your understanding of God, and of the teacher as shepherd?

8

The teacher as warrior

I think you know that part of my job is to train students to become teachers. In my university, we also provide advanced and other in-service courses for experienced teachers, as well as the higher degrees and research studies for which some teachers also enrol. That all means that I have to do quite a lot of talking to teachers. I also have to listen to them, for that's important too.

I've been doing those things with much pleasure for a long time. But now there's a difference. Yes, I know that things are bound to change over a period of time, and teacher-talk is no exception. Many of the problems teachers raise are the same as I raised as a young teacher thirty-odd years ago, in my first teaching post. But some teachers now talk about their job in a new and disturbing way. I've collected many such comments in the last two or three years. Here's a brief selection from that list for you to consider.

139

First, here's a primary-school teacher from Bishop Auckland. 'My workload as teacher and deputy head increases rapidly, and the behaviour and problems of the children are both appalling. They're so unruly and aggressive.'

Next a teacher from an Inner London comprehensive school. 'Where I teach, man, it's war. It's us versus them – all the time.'

Now for another deputy head from a school on the Lancashire coast. 'I hope you teach your students to be physically fit as well as good at their subjects, because they'll need to be tough if they come to teach in our schools.'

And what about this from a head of English in a Birmingham school. 'All our lessons are double sessions of seventy minutes. It takes twenty minutes to settle them, they switch off for the last part, and so with luck we teach for the rest. We most of us think we've been successful if we can keep them busy and quiet for twenty minutes or so.'

What about the newspapers? Have you seen the educational headlines lately? Here are two recent ones from the English press. One read: TEACHER UP FOR ASSAULT ON THIRTEEN-YEAR-OLD. Apparently this child had attacked his teacher, who retaliated in self-defence, and the parents took him to court.

The other headline shouted: MAYHEM IN (MIDDLE-TOWN) – SIX-YEAR-OLDS RUN RIOT. The article which followed described how, in one primary school, five- and six-year-olds were so undisciplined that they raced round their classroom, throwing everything they could find all over the place. They then charged out into the play-ground, leaving their helpless teacher in tears. Yes, that's right. The children concerned weren't teenagers. They were no more than six years of age. Six. I ask you. What on earth could have brought them to do that?

I wonder what you think about all these things – the teachers' comments, and the news items? It's enough to make any would-be teacher train to be a librarian or an accountant. Perhaps people like me should stop teaching courses in educational philosophy and learning theory and replace them with sessions on military strategy. Perhaps we should scrap our university teaching resources centre, and replace it with an army assault course.

Yes, I know – and you know as well – that not all schools and all children are like that. There are many, many schools where successful teaching and learning take place every day. But things *have* changed. Teaching *is* harder now than it used to be. There are far more problem pupils today. They're more aggressive, defiant and self-willed. They are simply part of the modern-day society which produced them. And as every Bible-loving Christian knows, all children have the potential to be like that. There is in every child's make-up that which would test, challenge and destroy, as well as that which will accept, support and encourage.

Many teachers do have a battle on their hands. But this should come as no surprise to any Christian. For every Christian has enlisted in an army. God's army. For the Christian who teaches, it's not just a struggle with unruly or disobedient pupils. They are only one aspect of the problem. In fact, if you were teaching in the pleasantest, most orderly school in the land, you would still have a major battle to engage in.

Christian warfare

Christian teachers *are* warriors. I'd be surprised if it occurred to most teachers to think of themselves like that as they walk into school each morning. But they should. And I believe that the Bible not only encourages us to see ourselves like that but also offers some pretty useful advice to keep us on the right course in the fight before us.

For example, in 2 Corinthians 10, Paul writes as follows:

> *For though we live in the world, we do not wage war as the world does. The weapons we fight with are not the weapons of the world. On the contrary, they have divine power to demolish strongholds. We demolish arguments and every pretension that sets itself up against the knowledge of God, and we take captive every thought to make it obedient to Christ (2 Corinthians 10:3–5).*

There are a lot of important points in those verses. They tell us we are at war, and must fight, and where. There are tactics and weapons to use, and some to avoid using. We're not just part of a defensive force; we must attack, and there are prisoners to take. And *we* have the power to win.

I know Paul probably had his preaching ministry principally in mind when he wrote those words. Nevertheless I believe their relevance to the teaching situation is very clear. So with the Holy Spirit's help, let's look at all the points Paul refers to, and see how they apply to teachers. I'll begin with the place of battle.

The battleground

We have to fight where we live. And we live in the world. Come off it, you say, that's obvious. Yes, it is. So obvious that it's very easy to forget it altogether. At least I often forget the fact. I'm much blessed. I live in a nice home with a super wife. I have an interesting job and lots of good friends. You may be able to say similar things. But we still live in the *world*. If our place of work happened to be a night club, or the race track, or a gambling casino, a pub or a dance hall, we'd be very much aware of being in the world. We'd be surrounded by some of the world's favourite values.

We'd probably be very uncomfortable most of the time, like Lot in Sodom. But schools are not like that. Are they? Oh yes, they are. They're as much in the world as any of these place. The world's standards and values permeate them too. But usually more subtly, and less obviously. Therefore more dangerously.

Remember we Christians are privileged people. We are not *of* the world. But as long as we are alive, we're in it, wherever we are and whatever we do. So school is as much a battleground for the Christian teacher, as the race track is for the Christian jockey.

Battle tactics

So we're in the world, but we don't wage war as the world does. A couple of chapters further on in his letter, Paul indicates some of the world's fighting methods. He does this when he expresses the fear that among the Corinthians he might find 'quarrelling, jealousy, outbursts of anger, factions, slander, gossip, arrogance and disorder' (2 Corinthians 12:20). All these can be found in schools and colleges, as can the suppression and watering down of the truth, cruelty, sarcasm, indifference and dislike. You know only too well that the people of this world, adults and children alike, use all these strategies from time to time in order to have their own way or come out on top. To be honest, some of us Christians act like that also, occasionally. It's all too easy, alas, to fall into the trap of using the same methods and weapons as those who are outside the Christian camp.

I once taught – thankfully for only a year or so – in

143

a school where a large group of the staff ganged up against the senior science master. At least once or twice a week, you could go into the staffroom and find several of the male teachers talking about him, always in terms of scorn and dislike. Not all the teachers would join in this regular character assassination, but many of them supported the attitudes of the main group, and tolerated what went on.

As it happens, they did have some cause for criticism, because this teacher was rather aloof and very sharp-tongued. And he did think his own views were always the right ones – and said so (which is never easy for those of us who know we're always right!). But he was also a very efficient teacher, always up to date with his marking and record-keeping. He did frequently give up some of his own time to help older pupils who were trying out experiments in the science laboratory, and he regularly helped his classes to gain good grades. He'd been at the school for some years, as also had his chief critics. So they'd all had plenty of time occasionally to get on one another's nerves.

As a new colleague, I was encouraged also to dislike and criticize him. But for the most part I was happily excluded from these awful backbiting sessions because of my newness. I hope also it was because they knew I would not take part with them. I admit I did not really like the man – he was not easy to love – but he always treated me courteously, on the rare occasions we spoke together.

I could never really understand why these colleagues wasted so much time attacking this man. Sadly, they seemed to enjoy doing so. It was only at the end of my first year in the school that I realized the motives of at least of two his detractors. I guess it'll come as no surprise to you to learn that one of the issues behind the scenes was internal promotion to a post of special responsibility. But there was also the malice which wanted to attack a disliked but successful fellow human being, plus the desire for cheap popularity by associating with those who opposed him.

Paul listed eight worldly weapons in that verse from 2 Corinthians 12. They were all there in that school situation, being used with deadly effect.

I've also experienced the situation where a small group of colleagues get together in clandestine fashion, to plan how to get their own way in changing school policy, or the curriculum, or the distribution of administrative chores. In all respects, they relied upon underhand tactics, and the general good nature of the rest of the teaching staff, to achieve their ends. Once again, the familiar tactics of the world, weapons used for selfish ends.

What would *you* do, if this happened in your school or college? Perhaps a more pointed question might be: What would you or I have done if we'd been among those in line for that school post of special responsibility with its extra pay and status? Or if we were of those likely to suffer from a changed timetable or extra duties? You'd probably have recognized the motives of those two other candidates and of the secret group more quickly than I did. So what Christian weapons would you have used in those circumstances?

The weapons to use

One thing is for sure. They certainly shouldn't be the weapons of the world. As a teacher, Paul, in his Corinthian letters, especially, rejects such approaches as clever and eloquent language, arguments based on worldly wisdom, impressive presentations and persuasive advertising. He also utterly repudiates the weapon of self-assertion in all its many blunt and subtle forms.

145

My own view is that he was not against eloquence and good presentation in themselves. The problem with weapons like these is that they can impress and persuade by their own character and style. They are too self-conscious, too attractive in themselves. The listener, the pupil if you like, is swayed by the techniques rather than by the message that the techniques are used to convey. Such weapons advertise themselves and the user more than the content to be taught. Hence success in those who respond is usually temporary, because the response is superficial rather than genuine and lasting. I've known teachers who use these weapons. Their success was all too often only skin deep.

Christian weapons

So what are the weapons that the Christian teacher should use? I know that in Ephesians 6, Paul describes the armour that God wants us to wear. In that passage, the only attacking weapon mentioned is the sword of the Spirit, which is the Word of God. Your speech should be seasoned with the salt of the Word, and you have every right, wherever you teach, to use it in your classroom, in the staffroom and school grounds, and with individuals as well as groups.

But you're probably not a Scripture teacher. And you're certainly not placed in your school to preach. So quoting from the Bible is hardly likely in most of your lessons, even though you might draw on that source for an example or an illustration occasionally. So how can you wage Christian warfare in your situation?

Well, the Christian does have other weapons to use. The Sermon on the Mount suggests several. Humility, for example. Showing mercy. Purity of heart. Peace-making. There are four really powerful ones for you. All four help to make you a better teacher, and a more influential one. Students are attracted both to you and to what you teach when they know you demonstrate true integrity and genuine concern for others rather than for yourself. And in the use of all these weapons you are witnessing to Christ. The real question for you and me is: Do we really believe all this?

A friend of mine was once questioned by one of his pupils on the subject of mercy. The conversation went like this:

'Sir, you're supposed to be a good Christian, aren't you?'

'Well, I'm a Christian, but not a very good one.'

'Well, then, sir, aren't Christians supposed to be merciful?'

'Yes, they are.'

'Then why did you keep us in last week for not working properly? Surely, you should be forgiving to us, because we're not all that old and wise.'

'Not at all. If I'd been a better Christian, I'd have kept you in for much longer than I did.'

He then explained that true justice and mercy don't turn a blind eye to wrongdoing, and that Christian mercy and Christian love are always present in just punishment.

The weapon of righteousness

I reckon that was a good blow for the cause of righteousness. Of course, righteousness itself is another very powerful weapon the Christian can use. Paul, earlier in his second letter to the Corinthians, specifically mentions the fact when he is describing how God's servants commend themselves to others. He refers to endurance, hardships and sufferings of various kinds, and hard work, and then says:

. . . in purity, understanding, patience and kindness; in the Holy Spirit and in sincere love; in truthful speech and in the power of God; with weapons of righteousness in the right hand and the left (2 Corinthians 6:6–7).

You know, when you stop to think about it – or rather to consult the Scriptures about it – we Christians have a whole arsenal of weapons to use. I'm afraid I often forget this, partly because of my own inadequacy as a Christian, but also because it's very difficult to measure success in the use of these weapons. For the most part, none of us ever sees their effects in any way that we could meaningfully assess. In any case, if you're like me, you're too concerned with your weak faith and cold heart, and your failure to show forth Christ in your life, to be able to understand how the Holy Spirit uses through you the weapons of God. Nevertheless, they are there for us to use.

I've already mentioned quite a few, but, praise God, there are more to come. Jesus commanded us to be as wise as serpents but as harmless as doves. Paul develops that in the passage we're looking at. He actually begins the chapter where these verses occur with an appeal which is 'by the meekness and gentleness of Christ' (2 Corinthians 10:1). Those are splendid weapons for the Christian. We too should fight by using them, in the power of Christ.

A young teacher's example

Take the story of thirteen-year-old Jason. One morning, he was absent from his school in downtown Bristol. That's because he was at the local police station, being questioned about an off-licence robbery the night before. As it happens, he wasn't involved, though he could have been. He was allowed to leave, and arrived at school half way through his Christian maths teacher's lesson.

Full of anger and resentment, he stormed into the classroom, brushed past the teacher and slumped down in his chair. 'Get out your maths book and look at the examples on page 59', he was instructed.

For an answer, he took out a huge flick-knife, opened the blade and stabbed it into the desk. The teacher looked at the quivering knife and repeated her request quietly but firmly. 'Get lost', he said. 'Why should I?'

She went up to him and stood in front of him. By this time, the whole class was on tenterhooks, watching to see what would happen. The teacher said, 'Come on, Jason, you know why. This work is important for you all, you included. And anyway, I'm your teacher, and I've asked you to do it.'

Then, to everyone's amazement, including Jason's, she gently pulled the knife out of the desk, opened the lid, and said, 'You get your book, and I'll keep this for you till the end of the lesson. Thank you for your co-operation.' Then she walked back to the front of the class and went on with her teaching.

She confessed later that she was scared stiff, especially when she took the knife. No pupil would have dared to do that to Jason. But she got away with it. Jason's attitude didn't change much, but at least he made a nominal show of doing the work she had asked him to do.

I believe this story is a good example of the meekness and gentleness of Christ in action. This is no soft or wet approach. She was quiet and gentle in both tone and manner, but showed the firmness and care that underlie those qualities. She did not bluster, threaten, or pull rank offensively. Nor did she make a great drama out of the incident. What she said was simple, and to the point. Everything was done quietly, and with no fuss. What else can I say but 'Hallelujah'?

The weapon of love

Jesus also commanded us to love, and that's the best weapon of all. Listen to another teacher:

The school in which I was teaching had to close. So, along with three other colleagues, I was transferred to teach in another establishment. I hated it from the very beginning. I used to come home every evening like a bear with a sore head. I took out my frustrations and anger upon my wife and children. I really was awful to live with. And this went on for nearly three years. I hated the school, I hated the kids, I hated the area, I hated even the school fabric. It was dreadful.

I could not understand why God had allowed this to happen to me. So I prayed about it, day after day. With my wife's help, I prayed for the kids to be changed. I prayed for the school to be improved. I prayed for the area to change. And nothing happened.

After a long time the Lord began to answer my prayers. But I did not at all like what he was saying to me. He wasn't going to take me to a more congenial school where I could work well for Him. Nor was he going to change everything in the school. What He told me was that I had to change, not everything else. He told me to ask him for a love of everything I hated. I had to ask for love for the kids, my colleagues, the school, the area, the lot. That was hard. Very hard. But when I asked, He gave.

Now I like those kids. Now at last, I can get down to their level. Jesus told me, 'I died for your sins and for theirs. I'm down there among them and among all their sin. You must come down there with me.' You see, in my utter ignorance and selfishness, I just did not understand. Now I can't wait for the new term to start. And there are so many involvements for the Lord. He makes things happen every day. I can still hardly believe it. It's great.

I find that testimony deeply moving, and very humbling as well. This same teacher also made another perceptive comment about witnessing for Christ in the classroom. He remarked, 'If kids can see the Lord clearly only in church, they'll never see Him, because most of them wouldn't be seen dead in church. So how can they ever know Him in the depths of their need and sin and misery if Christians don't show His love in school?'

It is hard to love every student you teach, and every colleague you work with. But Jesus *will* help you, especially with the difficult cases. You've just got to let Him work on you and in you, so that He can then work through you. The world has no effective answer to love, no effective defence against it. That's hardly surprising when you think about it. After all, it needs love more than anything else.

The weapon of truth

The other obvious weapon of the Christian teacher is truth. We, more than any others, stand for the truth. As teachers – and this really applies to everyone who teaches – we represent truth to our students, both in what we teach them and in how we live. As Christ himself pointed out, it is the truth that makes people free (John 8:32). Your pupils can come to realize this eventually for themselves. How? By the way you

151

represent truth and the way you teach your portion of it.

The targets to attack

Right. Now we know our weapons, we have to ask, 'On what do we use them?' Again, I'd like to remind you that the approach you have to adopt is an attacking one. You have a demolition job to do as well as a building task. Part of your duty as a teacher is to confront the wisdom of this world, and, where it conflicts with the teaching of Christ – for example, in moral understanding and in values education – demolish the strongholds of error and doubt.

One such stronghold is that of arguments or reasonings against Christian truth and the knowledge of God. I've always liked the King James Version's translation of that first bit of 2 Corinthians 10:5. It reads 'casting down imaginations'. The word used, *logismos*, means, 'a reasoning, a thought'. But the word 'imaginations' has the suggestion of intentions as well. And since many of our thoughts are the outcome of that creative faculty of the mind that we call our imagination, I think it no forcing of the text to suggest that Christian teachers must attack not just arguments but every thought, idea, and imagination of the heart which goes against Christian truth.

Now I have known some young Christian teachers who thought that witnessing in school consisted of winning arguments about Christianity. They would gladly set up situations when discussion of Christian truths could take place. Such approaches are not usually of much help. Let an experienced primary teacher make the reply. She said to me once, 'Situations must come naturally so that we respond in the same way.' Engineering situations so that you can speak of the Lord is usually of the flesh, not the Spirit. Too often they are artificial. They usually prompt the same old questions: 'Why does a good God allow cancer? Or the holocaust?' I find these very hard to answer convincingly. But the main trouble is that they are mere intellectual difficulties. They are not felt personally by the one who raises them. It is the *personal* need, when it is expressed, that enables real witnessing to be done.

Paul says that the other key target to attack is 'every pretension which sets itself up against the knowledge of God' 'Every high thing that exalteth itself against the knowledge of God', as the KJV puts it.

I guess you'll ask, 'How does this apply to the ordinary Christian teacher, who teaches not theology or religious education, but history, geography, science, literature, music, or physical education?' Well, what you have to do is to study the material you have to teach, along with any textbooks available for your pupils. If you find – and I'm pretty sure you will – ideas, stories, examples or values which contradict biblical teaching, then you must be ready to expose them for the sham that they are. The same is true of thoughts and ideas put forward by your pupils. My friend's example about 'being merciful' is an illustration of that.

I'm not able to give you detailed analysis of all the material we teachers are expected to put over to our classes. But I can suggest a few ideas to start you thinking. I guess you'll be ready to supply many more from your own experience.

1. Science. Very common is the idea that scientific knowledge, *i.e.* knowledge arrived at by empirical investigation, is the only true kind. It's supposed to be truly objective. Subjective knowledge is discounted. Yet knowledge which comes from, and only from, commitment of the self to another person – or to a poem, or

153

piece of music – is just as valid and genuine. Indeed, without such personal involvement, that knowledge will never be gained. If you're not sure about this, just ask yourself how far you'd get with the person you'd like to marry if you confined your knowledge of him or her to what you could discover by scientific tests only.

2. *History*. History textbooks abound with suggestions that man is the arbiter of his own destiny, that man is the measure of all things. These secular humanist ideas can easily be shown to be false. They must be, if students are not to leave school with erroneous views about man's past and possible future. That's not to say you must simply teach the Christian view of history. But your students in all fairness should at least know what this view is, along with the others.

3. *The arts*. There are many wrong values, ideas and prejudices propounded in literature, music and art. You owe it to your students to set these values against Christian understanding and standards. For example, the notions of freedom of expression and artistic licence, which allow anything to be said and done in the cause of art and so-called greater realism, need exposing and countering.

4. *Geography*. We need to beware of the implicit racism of some descriptions of human geography, and in demographic studies.

5. *Physical education*. We also need to alert our students to that worship of physical fitness which is one of the main idolatries of our time. Bodily exercise does have some profit, as Paul himself acknowledged. But it is not the only or the ultimate way to health and success. Watching with the sincerest pity exhausted joggers stag-

gering around the Capitol on a sticky-hot Washington lunch-hour in the height of summer, I longed to quote St Paul to them. Of course, I didn't dare. So I just prayed they'd not have heart attacks.

6. Moral education. Christian teachers need to stand out against harsh or petty rules. They must oppose discrimination against certain groups or individuals. They must resist unfair rewards and punishments, undue favouritism, and so on. And if your school teaches values clarification in its personal and social education course, for instance, then beware the biased and highly unsatisfactory nature of many of the ideas and examples advocated by those who write textbooks and teacher aids in this area.

The captives to take

Paul reminds us that we're in the business of taking prisoners as well. And this, for me, is the hardest part. He says we must take captive every thought to make it obedient to Christ. Did you get that? He said: *Every* thought. Capturing and subduing other people's thoughts is hard enough. But every thought includes my thoughts too. And, oh dear, that's a massive problem in itself. You may well find it easier to attack false idols like worldly knowledge and values, occult pretensions, or the modern gods of self, human intellect, majority opinion, 'the experts' and so on.

But Paul says we must take every thought captive. We can begin to do that only in the power of Christ. No wonder the Lord keeps urging us constantly to watch and pray. Teachers are in the business of purveying ideas, and helping children to think and use their minds as fully as possible. As we submit *our* minds to the Lordship of Christ, so we shall be more able to take our thoughts and our teaching of the ideas of others into the perspective of Jesus. Whether your pupils accept or reject this perspective, at least they will have been made aware of its demands on them, in all aspects of their education.

A note of encouragement

Are you thoroughly daunted by all this? You might well react by saying that you'll certainly try your best to teach and witness faithfully, but you'd prefer others, abler or better than you think you are, to do the front-line attacking. Let them go out of the trenches first. It's an attitude I readily share, because I know my limitations too.

But, you know, that's the whole point. I'll never succeed in my own strength and my own limited knowledge. Neither will you. God knows this even better than we do. That's why He wants us to use His weapons and not the weapons of the world. If you live by the standards of this world, you will surely fail. But, as Paul says, we *don't* live by this world's precepts and values. We *don't* wage war as the world does.

We have weapons which have *divine* power to demolish strongholds. Using the weapons of Christ successfully does not depend on *our* ability and *our* wisdom and expertise. It rests on our faith and our obedience. Once more we come back to the words of the old hymn: 'Trust and obey, for there's no other way . . .'. He's given us the ability to teach, and He's put us where we are to do just that. So we naturally just go forward day by day, trusting Him to use us as He sees fit. The power is not in us, but in the meekness and gentleness of Christ, in love, in truth, in mercy, righteousness, purity of heart and peacemaking. They are the means not merely to batter at strongholds, but actually to demolish them.

Think about Jason and his mathematics teacher again for a moment. In human terms, the teacher was on a hiding to nothing. Jason was a tearaway. He was known to be capable of violence, a law-breaker, a delinquent. He could easily have made mincemeat of his teacher. And yet he didn't. His encounter with the police that morning had clearly raised strong feelings of anger and resentment. Yet he did not react like that to his teacher. Why not?

There can only be one answer. The weapons the teacher used, Christian weapons, demolished by the grace of God the strongholds of bitterness, violence and disobedience. And remember that she would use these weapons consistently in her teaching. She admitted later how scared she was. She also said she'd have had no idea what to do if Jason had defied her or become aggressive. All she could do, and all she did, was to act as she thought right and best – as any teacher, especially a Christian teacher, should. Divine power did the rest. I said it before, and I unhesitatingly say it again: 'Hallelujah.'

Our task is to get on with the job, in faith. We will almost certainly have to endure hardship as good soldiers of Christ, as Paul advised Timothy. Also, no-one serving as a soldier gets involved in civilian affairs – he wants to please his commanding officer (2 Timothy 2:4). So we need to watch, and pray, and to keep ourselves from idols and from being polluted by the world.

In everything we can be sure of one fact. Victory is ours. Jesus says: 'Take heart! I have overcome the world' (John 16:33). 'This is the victory that has overcome the world, even our faith' (1 John 5:4).

For prayer and discussion

1. Look up Ephesians 6:10–19, and meditate on the various items of spiritual armour listed there. How will each piece help you in your daily life as a teacher?

2. Examine 1 Thessalonians 5:4–11, if possible with at least one other Christian teacher. Follow the advice given in verse 11, in relation to the teacher as a soldier of Christ.

3. The hymnwriter, referring to the Ephesians passage, wrote, 'Each piece put on with prayer.' Spend some time alone, and also with others, praying about your work and armour, in the light of the struggle against the forces of darkness.

4. There are a number of other references in the Bible to spiritual armour and weaponry. Using a concordance, look up these verses and consider how they reinforce what this chapter has said on the subject.

5. Why not also, as I have done, ask around among other Christian teachers you know for examples from their experience of how God led and helped them in particular situations at school. You'll find that yet another tremendous encouragement to you.

9

The teacher as fragrance

I don't know about you but I really like going to conferences, especially those for Christian teachers. There's something very special about meeting other Christians who do the same kind of work as you do. You can share your problems, listen to their experiences, and swap ideas. I recommend it to you.

I remember driving to one of these conferences in the south of England several years ago. The convention was taking place in an area I was not familiar with, and I took a wrong turn and lost my way. The organizers had sent me a map. But I confess I'm not always very good at following such directions, even when I have my wife with me to try to keep me right, I like to think I've memorized them. I certainly try, in order to avoid having to keep stopping for another look. And so I drive on and hope for the best. Alas, I should know better because sooner or later I find I'm in the wrong place and then I have to stop and start looking all over again.

Well, this time I had been too clever as usual and was lost. I knew from signs I'd seen that I was pretty close to the college where the meetings were being held. Then I saw a group of teenagers, so I got out of the car, crossed over to them, and asked for directions, which they gave me. As I turned to go back to the car, one boy called out, 'What do you want to go there for? It's holiday time and it'll be closed.'

I explained about the conference, and he asked me what it was about. So I told him it was a meeting of Christian teachers and lecturers who would be coming from all parts of the country. I'll not forget his reply. 'Huh!' he said. 'Rather you than me. I think Christians stink, and teachers stink even worse.'

Unfortunately neither of us had time to take this further, so we went our separate ways. But I can still hear him saying it, and his friends laughing as he did so.

What I was not able to tell him then was that, although he did not realize it, he was, as far as Christians are concerned, uttering a profound theological truth. And it's a truth that should give every Christian teacher a lot of encouragement. If you don't believe me, have a look at chapter 2 of Paul's second letter to the Corinthians. Paul doesn't quite phrase it as my young friend did, nor does he make the comment with the negative vehemence I experienced, but the basic point is the same. Consider what Paul writes:

But thanks be to God, who always leads us in triumphal procession in Christ and through us spreads everywhere the fragrance of the knowledge of him. For we are to God the aroma of Christ among those who are being saved and those who are perishing. To the one we are the smell of death; to the other, the fragrance of life. And who is equal to such a task? Unlike so many, we do not peddle the word of God for profit. On the contrary, in Christ we speak before God with sincerity, like men sent from God (2 Corinthians 2:14–17).

Look at those verses again. We are the aroma of Christ, he says. To one kind of people, those who are perishing, we are the smell of death (we stink!). To the other kind, those who are being saved, we are the fragrance of life.

Now may I ask you a question? Have you ever stopped to think about that idea at all? I confess I've read that passage many times, but only recently did the Lord make me sit up and take real notice of it. And, not surprisingly, I found that the idea is well worth examining more closely. If you consider it carefully, I think you'll find it'll act like a tonic to give you more heart for your Christian witness in school.

A sweet savour

As you've discovered by now, I'm interested in meanings and definitions. I suppose it comes from my once being a teacher of English. I like to know the exact sense of particular words, if at all possible. And also any related meanings and overtones. Of course, to know precisely what a word literally means is a special help when studying the Word of God. It's good to know what God is specifically saying at each point in the message. So let's quickly glance at this word, which in verses 14 and 16 is translated 'fragrance' or 'sweet savour'. The Greek word used here is *osmē*, which simply means 'smell', 'odour'. But in the context of the passage here, it more particularly means 'an odour accompanying an acceptable sacrifice'.

Have you ever been camping by a lake or in the country? Perhaps, when it was time for a meal, you collected some dried grasses and dead wood and started a fire, so that you could have a steak fry with onions. Perhaps you've walked along an English street early in the morning when people are making breakfast, and permeating the air is a delicious smell of rich, smoked bacon. Maybe you've barbecued hamburgers in the garden on a summer evening. Or you may even have been lucky enough, like me, to visit friends in Wisconsin, USA, where they organize cook-outs to grill those juicy, tasty bratwurst sausages they like so much. If you've experienced any of these things, then you'll know exactly what idea this word would conjure up for those who first read this letter of Paul's. They wouldn't know about steak fries, cook-outs or English bacon, but they would know about burnt offerings. If you glance back at the book of Leviticus, there's a lot about burnt offerings there. Repeated again and again is the description of these as a sweet savour acceptable to the Lord.

The Israelites were commanded to offer their sacrifices on the altar, and the scent of the burnt offerings would be a sweet smell pleasing to God. That's what the word means here. The loveliest example of all of the use of this word in the Bible can be found in Ephesians 5:2, where we read that Christ 'gave himself up for us as a fragrant offering and sacrifice to God'.

Have you ever thought of yourself like that? Paul says that we Christians are to God the aroma of Christ. A fragrant offering. A sweet savour indeed. How about that? I guess you don't usually picture yourself in that way as you walk into school at the start of a new day. It's possible you've heard the same kind of comment that that youth made to me as I looked for the way to the conference centre. You certainly know he wasn't being complimentary about teachers or Christians. But this passage of Scripture says you are a sweet fragrance, and that some people – and this will include some of your pupils – will regard you in that way rather than as that teenager did. Isn't that worth thinking about? Let's ponder the idea together and see what comes out of it.

I'd like to draw your attention to three facts or qualities about fragrance that will help you and challenge you as a Christian teacher. Two we'll look at straight away. The third I'll hold over till near the end.

Fragrance is indispensable

If something has a scent, that scent usually expresses the essence, the main distinguishing characteristic of that thing. Its intrinsic nature, its indispensable quality, is bound up in that scent or perfume. The obvious example is a flower. In the natural world, colour and scent are the two most important features of many plants and flowers. Both are essential to their survival in the wild, but the scent is probably the more important because it draws attention to the plant's presence, even when the plant itself can't be seen. Not all flowers are distinctively scented, but those that are owe their attractive aroma to the presence on their petals of essential oils. It is a remarkable fact that only a minute quantity of these essential oils is sufficient to produce the scent. It has been estimated that even in the most heavily perfumed flower, the essential oils never make up more than 2% of the floral plant material. Only a very small amount has a very big impact.

I love roses. They are my favourite above all. I know that modern gardening techniques have produced great numbers of different varieties, and that some of these hybrids have no noticeable scent at all. But the old-fashioned roses, and some of the new ones also, have the loveliest of fragrances. Or what about lilac, or honeysuckle, or jasmine, especially on a warm late spring evening? Super. In every case, their scent comes from the very heart of their being. Some you can detect from a distance, while with others, the violet for instance, you have to come very close to discern that distinctive sweetness. Their fragrance expresses what most makes the flowers what they truly are.

Christians, including Christian teachers, are like that too. With some, their singular nature is obvious. But with a great many more, you can't always tell straight away what their special fragrance is. The danger is that people will judge too readily that they have no fragrance at all. But the pupils of Christian teachers will know.

Let me illustrate this with a personal example. One Saturday morning I asked my wife if there was anything I could do for her. I was rather hoping for a quiet time, but as any husband will tell you, to ask your wife a question like that is fatal. She immediately found me a job. 'Yes dear,' she said. 'Will you just tidy the front room for me, please?'

So I armed myself with a duster and set off to do as she asked. As I was dusting and replacing some ornaments on a shelf, I came across a pretty dish which had some mouldy-looking dust in it. I took the dish to my wife, to show her. 'You'll not want this awful-looking stuff, will you? I can't imagine what it's doing there.'

'No, no, don't throw it away,' she replied. 'Just take a pinch between your fingers and rub it.' So I did. And the most beautiful aroma at once came from the 'dust'. It was dried lavender. It looked dead and dirty. But it was lovely.

I wonder if you're a bit like that? Don't get me wrong. I am not for a moment suggesting that you look either dead or dirty. But it is possible that you may regard yourself as ordinary, undistinguished, and nothing special. At first glance, others who do not know you might think of you like that as well. But these words in 2 Corinthians categorically remind you that you're not like that at all. You are special, and your special fragrance underlines this. As a born-again Christian, you have at the very heart of you the Lord Jesus who dwells in you by His Spirit. At the centre of your being there is the aroma of Christ. You may well not be conscious of your own special scent. I don't mean that you are unaware that God the Holy Spirit dwells in your heart. Not at all. I'm sure you know that your body is a temple of the living God. But I'd be surprised if you were fully aware of that particularly lovely fragrance which is you. It *is* there, all right. Take God's word for it.

And even though you may not be cognisant of its existence, everyone who comes into direct contact with you certainly will be. Many will not know or understand, or be able to identify it correctly,. But they'll know. And that brings me to the second characteristic of fragrance.

Fragrance communicates

Fragrance makes its presence known. In a way, it can't help itself. You may be walking down a country lane near a bank awash with bluebells. You may be passing a crofter's cottage on a crisp morning in the Scottish highlands as the smoke from his peat fire curls from the chimney. You may call on a friend just as the coffee begins to percolate. Or you may be out in your garden and catch the scent of woodsmoke as a neighbour sets fire to dead twigs and other garden rubbish. In each case you catch the fragrance in your nostrils. It has told you it is there.

I had a particularly strong reminder of this self-evident fact the other day, when a teacher in her early thirties came to see me. She wanted to read for a PhD and had made an appointment to consider with me the field of study in which she wished to do her research. We had a useful session and she went away satisfied with the suggestions we had discussed. But all the time she was in my room, I was conscious of the perfume she was wearing. It was pleasant enough, but in my private opinion, I thought she'd overdone it and put too much on. To be honest, it was a bit overpowering. It certainly made me aware of its presence.

Now I know that this fact about scent and perfume is blatantly obvious. Of course it communicates. It would be utterly useless if it didn't. But apply this truth to the Christian and you'll find a great many of the Lord's people to whom it has never occurred. They've never realized that they are the aroma of Christ and that that aroma conveys itself to others just like any other fragrance. They wouldn't think twice about the fact where perfume or the scent of a day lily is concerned. But they do need reminding about the sweet savour of Christ – *in them*!

When Christian teachers walk into their classroom, or the staffroom, they bring Christ with them. Wherever we go, the Lord is with us. Now I'm sure that you wouldn't go into your school each day unprepared for the work ahead. You'll have spent some time – for certain lessons, a very great deal of time – planning what to do and how to do it. Well, why not spend some preparation time on how to communicate the aroma of Christ more effectively? You'll quickly find that preparation for good teaching, and planning to spread the fragrance of the Lord, are usually one and the same, involving study and prayer. You know only too well that most students will not learn much at all if you just give them the lesson material and leave them to get on with it as best they can. Why therefore leave your scent bottle corked? It is still possible to get some idea of a particular fragrance by holding the bottle close to your nose and breathing in deeply. But unscrew the stopper, and, oh, what a great aroma! You get the full message this time, and you're in no doubt about the kind of fragrance contained in it.

So how do you communicate the aroma of Christ in your school? You enable it to get its message across in three main ways. They're all simple and straightforward, just like unscrewing a stopper, so there's no need to feel in any way apprehensive.

The fragrance of speech

Let's deal with the most obvious way first. We can do it very briefly, since it has already been the subject of an earlier chapter. Your special kind of fragrance comes through very clearly both in what you say and how you say it. I know a head teacher who, when he is inter-viewing prospective teachers for a post on the staff of his school, almost always sets up a role-play situation for the candidates. He makes them imagine they are in a particular classroom setting. Then, using himself and whoever else is on the panel of interviewers as 'pupils', he asks each candidate to 'teach' them in some way. One of his favourite scenes is a situation requiring disciplinary action on the teacher's part. He claims that it's a really good way to find out about the personality and potential of those being interviewed.

I'm not at all sure I'd ever want to apply for a job in his school.. I'd be delighted to work with him. It's the interview that I'd not much care to experience. Never-theless, you can see his point. As he himself comments, 'You can tell a great deal about someone by the language they use and the tone of voice they adopt.' His words certainly apply to any classroom, and most children and young people would agree with him. My younger daughter never liked school very much at any stage of her educational career. I've often wondered whether one reason was the bad year she had when she was only six years old, with a teacher none of her class liked. Jane dismissed her as 'a shouty teacher'. When asked to explain, she said, 'When she tells us to do anything, she always shouts. She's not a whispering voice at all.' I happen to know that many of that teacher's statements and comments were phrased in what could be described as hard language. Clearly her fragrance was not one that attracted her pupils.

Peter had a good word for all this. In his first letter, he wrote as follows: 'If anyone speaks, he should do it as one speaking the very words of God' (1 Peter 4:11). He was talking about using faithfully the gifts we have been given. Certainly those who are called to teach have been given a gift for speaking. If you exercise your gift in the way Peter describes, you will undoubtedly communicate the aroma of Christ to all who hear you.

When I was a very young teacher, I did not own a car, and so I had to travel fifteen miles each day by train from the town where we lived to the city centre where the school was situated. One of my favourite lessons was teaching poetry, and I used to be so glad of that journey when I had such a lesson to teach. Often, as I travelled, I would work out different wordings for my questions about the poems I had planned to read with the class. Or I'd practise various ways of explaining points in the poems. I'd do this because it is so easy to put pupils off poetry by phrasing questions and comments inappropriately. I was always concerned to ask those questions and say those things which would most help the class to appreciate the poem we were reading. Experience soon taught me that the words I used had to be exactly right if I was to succeed in my task. So that rehearsal of different wordings on the way to school proved invaluable.

I have to confess that I did not plan my choice of words for all the rest of my teaching, as I did for my poetry lessons. But I can say that I was usually more successful in giving my instructions to a class, or in praising or rebuking, when I'd thought hard about the actual expressions I was to use. Experience always helps of course, but finding the right words, and rehearsing how to say them, is well worth spending time over if you really want to achieve those high aims you have set for yourself and your pupils. It's not only Christian teachers who show this kind of professionalism, but the Christian who has such an approach 'to do all for the glory of God' certainly unstoppers the aroma of Christ.

I reckon that the real test of your ability to communicate that special Christian fragrance that is you, comes when under pressure. Things can go wrong even in the best prepared lessons. And discipline problems are bound to come your way from time to time. Not all the things we have to teach children are exciting and attention-riveting. And both you and your pupils get tired. What sort of words do you use then? Do they reveal the 'old man' still lurking in you, or the 'new man', the new creation you are in Christ Jesus? Likewise in the staffroom when you chat with your fellow teachers: do you gossip about that awkward colleague, and join in the criticism of the head? Or do you defend the weak, and speak up for what is right? What sort of fragrance *do* you communicate?

Don't be in any doubt at all. Whatever may appear to be the effect of your words, you will assuredly be conveying the aroma of Christ to all who hear you speaking what is good and true and lovely.

The fragrance of actions

The second obvious way in which you will communicate the sweet savour of the Lord is in what you do. How's this for a testimonial?

I went once to speak to a day conference of sixth-form students who were nearing the end of their school life. After my talk, the meeting broke up into groups, and I had a chance to speak to a number of individuals. Asking one group about their time at school, I found the conversation turned to some of their teachers. There were the usual disagreements. Some preferred this teacher. Some disliked that one. Then one girl, Mary, made a disparaging remark about their history teacher. Holy Joe, they called him. 'He's so fussy,' she complained. 'He's never satisfied until you get your references and quotations just right.'

Steve agreed. 'Yeah, he's pernickety. He's a bit boring as well sometimes. But I've had more help from him than anyone else in this school. When I first started to specialize in history, I used to get all mixed up. There's so much to read, and I didn't know where to start. He knew this and stayed back after school with me one afternoon and talked to me about my difficulties. He encouraged me to practise writing things down, which he'd then read for me, and he loaned me some of his own books. He spent a lot of his own time on me and really helped me. He never let on to anyone else about this, and I was grateful, because I didn't want you lot to know I was having those problems with my work.'

I liked that. One reason why I liked it was because, unknown to Steve and the others, I knew Holy Joe. He'd been on the staff of his school for many years. And he was a Christian. I suppose that's why they called him Holy Joe. Now you and I both know that there are dedicated non-Christian teachers in our schools who would do just what this man did for Steve. Even so, here was a Christian man doing his job thoroughly, demanding high standards from his students, but prepared to give up his own time, and books, to help when one of them needed him, and sensitive enough to save

170

the student's embarrassment by ensuring that no other student knew of this extra help he was giving. And this was to just one of the students he taught. I wondered how many other pupils in that school could reveal similar stories of his help and encouragement. His actions were conveying the aroma of Christ, quietly and without any publicity or drama.

In the letter to the Colossians, we read:

Slaves, obey your earthly masters in everything; and do it, not only when their eye is on you to win their favour, but with sincerity of heart and reverence for the Lord (Colossians 3:22).

Holy Joe didn't watch the clock so that he could rush away the moment school ended. He didn't teach with one eye on the head teacher or the senior master, so that he could gain human praise. He may not even have been the greatest of teachers, but he taught sincerely and with thoroughness – and this because he honoured his Lord. As the letter to the Ephesians puts it, following an injunction similar to the one from Colossians just quoted, 'Serve wholeheartedly, as if you were serving the Lord, not men' (Ephesians 6:7).

Effective communication of your fragrance means preparing your work effectively, being punctual for your lessons, not shirking your duties, keeping your reports up to date, doing your marking of pupils' work promptly, and so on. One of the best early lessons I had as a student teacher was being in a school where a general inspection was to take place. The week before the inspection was due to begin, there was an unusual hive of activity among certain members of the staff. Lesson notes appeared from nowhere, teaching aids that had gathered dust on the shelf were taken down and off to lessons, and piles of unmarked books suddenly

171

disappeared. I was asked to return one such pile to a class I was teaching. One boy remarked that it was the first time that year that they'd ever had anything back from that particular teacher. It was the look on this boy's face, and the attitude of his classmates to that teacher, that made me understand the kind of effect our actions (or lack of action) have on our students.

Your students will not always appreciate what you do for them, or why you do it. But the consistent, day-in, day-out, year-in, year-out conscientiousness you demonstrate will undoubtedly have a real effect for good. I know it's only doing your duty. But it is a powerful witness. And it will make an impression. You may well not be able to measure it, but that does not matter. After all, the one you are really working for is God Himself.

The fragrance of attitudes

Now let me tell you about Daniel Johnson. That's not his real name. He's a teacher I know. I first met him when he was a master's degree student on one of my courses. He's intelligent, lively, a good participant in discussion. He works hard, and he got on well with his fellow students on the course. All my colleagues who knew him agreed that he was just the sort of higher-degree candidate we wanted. And he proved us right by getting a very good degree at the end of the course. Not surprisingly, we all enjoyed having him in our classes, for he was genuinly interested in the study of education.

One reason why we accepted him to study with us was because of the references we received about him when we were first considering his application. His head teacher emphasized that he was very efficient, a meticulous teacher, thorough, reliable and hard-working. A model professional, in fact. Eighteen months after gaining his MA degree, I heard that he'd been promoted to the headship of a large comprehensive school in Manchester. I remember thinking how fortunate that school was. I said as much to one of his former colleagues when I happened to visit his old school where one of my students was doing his teaching practice. The teacher agreed. 'Yes, it's the ideal job for him,' he said. 'Administration is his best line.' And then he added, 'Teaching children was never really his kind of work. None of us was really sorry to see him go, you know. And the kids were delighted. They disliked him intensely.'

I was shocked, and said so. I described what a good student we had found him to be. 'Oh yes, he would be,' was the reply. 'But deep down, you know, he hated kids – and they knew it.'

Even now, many years later, I find that story disturbing and hard to believe. Yet it teaches me afresh that attitudes are so important, especially where children and young people are concerned. I just don't understand how Daniel Johnson could make teaching his career for so long – apparently he moved into educational administration from his headship – if he disliked the young so much. He set a good example in some things. But it seems that he could not disguise some of his basic reactions. Perhaps he did not realize that these attitudes inevitably reveal themselves sooner or later, and in doing so they also reveal the nature of their holder. They communicate the essential flavour of the person. It is in our attitudes that we Christians can most effectively communicate the aroma of Christ.

What sort of teachers do our children most need? That's easy. They need teachers who genuinely love them – not sentimentally, but with true care and compassion, a love based on respect for them as persons created by God in His image; teachers who enjoy their

173

subjects, who have a real enthusiasm for and commitment to what they teach; teachers who are patient and kind, not arrogant or self-opinionated, but who can be firm and gentle; tteachers who can be trusted, good and honourable men and women who stand for what is right; teachers who can discipline their classes in positive ways because *they* are self-diisciplined, in control of themselves.

Does that describe you? I see no reason at all why it should not do so. Read that last paragraph again. Does it not ring a bell somewhere in your mind? You've probably recognized already that I'm alluding to Galatians 5:22–23, those lovely verses about the fruit of the Spirit. It is the indwelling Spirit of God who creates in us these attitudes, and enables us to maintain and develop them – attitudes to our students, to our colleagues, to authority and to all our work. After all, 'in Christ we speak before God with sincerity, like men sent from God' (2 Corinthians 2:17).

And that's what you are. A person sent from God, to teach boys and girls. Do you know what that word 'sincerity' literally means? It means 'unsullied brightness'. As you teach day by day, with sincerity, so your Christian light will shine forth. And so also will the sweet savour of Christ be communicated to your pupils and your colleagues.

Problem time

It's at this point that you might well remember that cheery character we quoted at the start of this chapter. You know, the one who thought that Christians and teachers 'stink'. Where does he fit into all this, and the many like him? Well, we communicate the fragrance of Christ through our words, our actions and our attitudes. But that passage from 2 Corinthians 2 clearly states that

174

to those who are perishing, we are the smell of death. They are hardly likely to respond with shouts of joy to our teaching, are they? No, alas, I'm afraid they are not. Worse still, there are those in your classes who are antagonized by the presence of Christ in the classroom. They will sneer. They will rebel. They will disobey. They will be insolent. They will not listen. They will be negative in various ways. The more crystal-clear you are in allowing the light of Christ to shine through, the more some of your students will be antagonistic and difficult. (I am not saying that this is the explanation for every problem student reaction.) As Jesus reminded his disciples: 'In the world you will have trouble' (John 16:33). That's as true for Christians who teach as for any others.

Did I hear you murmur, 'And that's not the only problem'? You might well also be thinking; 'If I'm the fragrance of life to my pupils, what an awesome responsibility that is. Who am I to cope with that?' I agree with you. That's a very fair question.

St Paul, you remember, asked the very same question. He wrote: 'And who is equal to such a task?' (2 Corinthians 2:16). Well, there is a simple and straight answer to that. It is that *you are*. Yes, *you* are. So am I. What's that you're now asking? How are we equal to it? I can tell you gladly. And this time I have two answers for you.

Fragrance lingers

The first answer is to refer to a third fact or quality about fragrance. You'll remember I said early on that there were three. We've already examined the first two – that fragrance is indispensable, and that it communicates. The third triumphant fact is that fragrance lingers after we have gone. Do you recall that would-be PhD student I mentioned earlier in the chapter? You know, the one wearing a rather strong perfume? Well, for at least two hours after she had left my room, I could smell her perfume lingering in the air. Even with the window open, it stayed around for some time.

Now just apply that fact to yourself. The Word of God tells you that you are to God the aroma of Christ. You know perfectly well that perfume always tends to hang in the air even when the wearer has gone away. So I'm asking you to rejoice with me that your aroma, your fragrance, stays on in the classrooms where you teach. More important still, it stays on in the minds of your pupils. You·*do* have an effect on them – on *all* of them – whatever you might think. You can't measure that effect. Nor, in most cases, can you ever be really sure what it is. You may find that frustrating sometimes. But you've just got to live with the fact.

Therefore you simply have to trust God that it is so. Trust Him to use you. Trust Him to apply your particular fragrance. To let it work. To make it linger. He will do this for you. He has promised.

So much for answer number one. Now what about the second answer to the question, 'How are we equal to such a task?' Please look again at 2 Corinthians 2:14. It reads: 'But thanks be to God, who always leads us in triumphal procession in Christ and' (here it comes) 'through us spreads everywhere the fragrance of the knowledge of him.'

You see? You don't have to worry at all. You are not alone. This awesome responsibility is not wholly on your shoulders, as you were beginning to think. You may be the only Christian on the teaching staff of your school. You may feel at times that the task is beyond you, that you are too weak and ordinary to have any real effect for God. Doubt no more, and do not be afraid. Think of Moses. His opinion of himself was very low indeed. He thought he was useless for the task God wanted him to perform. I once read somewhere that Moses lived for 120 years. The first forty years he spent trying to be somebody. The next forty years he spent learning to be a nobody. The last forty years he spent showing what God can do with somebody who has learned to be a nobody – for God. He learned to stop thinking and worrying about himself by concentrating on God and what He wanted. And look at the effect he had – all because he allowed God to work in him and through him.

Now let's come back to you and your situation – and to 2 Corinthians 2:14. It is not you who spreads everywhere the fragrance of the knowledge of Christ. It is God. You are in *your* school because that's where God placed you. You are sent from God (2 Corinthians 2:17) into your present situation, whatever that it. And it is God who leads you in triumphal procession in Christ. Has that last bit registered? In *triumphal* procession. I know it doesn't seem like that for much of the time. But your fragrance, the aroma of Christ which demonstrates what you are in very essence, does communicate, every day, and does linger, does have an effect, does work the work that God has called you to perform for Him. All you and I have to do is, like Moses, to trust and obey.

Therefore . . . stand firm. Let nothing move you. Always give yourselves fully to the work of the Lord, because you know that your labour in the Lord is not in vain (1 Corinthians 15:58).

For prayer and discussion

1. Look up the first seven chapters of Leviticus and note the references to 'sweet savour'. Can you apply the teaching behind the offerings described to your own practice?

2. Pray that your Christian perfume is having a positive effect on your students, and your colleagues, and ask God to show you how this might be even more effective.

3. In what ways is the Christian the smell of death to those who are perishing and the fragrance of life to those being saved? Do your answers have any implications for *your* teaching witness?

4. Consider with other Christian teachers how to develop and demonstrate positive Christian attitudes in the exercise of discipline, the teaching of subject-matter, and inter-personal classroom relationships.

5. How might you more effectively help those pupils whom you find most difficult to like and to teach?

10

The teacher as teacher

My dear reader, if you've lasted this far, thank you. But you must be looking at the title of this chapter and asking yourself, 'What's it all about? Surely the whole book is to do with teaching. So why a special chapter?'

I want to begin with a confession. You know from the things I've said earlier that I've been teaching a long time. I still think I've much to learn, especially about being a Christian teacher. And I confess to you that as I open my Bible and read its different writings, and by the grace of God begin to glimpse how some of what is written applies to the teaching situation, I wish I'd realized these things years ago. I might have been a better teacher then, and now.

So I ask you straight away to strive to apply the Scriptures to your own personal teaching scene. Along with the Bible passages, I've tried to tell you lots of stories involving Christian teachers. It does help to know some of what others have experienced. But you are *you*, not them. Your situation is unique to you. God knows that best of all. He *will* help you to relate His truth to yourself and the school where He has placed you.

I know that the Bible is not just a pedagogical primer for would-be teachers. But I do believe utterly that the more you study it, with your personal teaching situation in mind, the more God will show you how His Word applies to you, there.

I've asked Him several times to give me a specific word for me as a teacher. He usually directs me to Paul's letters to Timothy. Let me give you an example.

Preach the Word; be prepared in season and out of season; correct, rebuke and encourage – with great patience and careful instruction. For the time will come when men will not put up with sound doctrine. Instead, to suit their own desires, they will gather around them a great number of teachers to say what their itching ears want to hear. They will turn their ears away from the truth and turn aside to myths. But you, keep your head in all situations, endure hardship, do the work of an evangelist, discharge all the duties of your ministry (2 Timothy 4:2–5).

It shouldn't take too much imagination to see how these words apply almost as much to your life as a teacher as they did to Timothy's life as an evangelist. They pretty well cover normal school life for us. So let's take a day in the life of a Christian teacher – you – and see how they fit everything you do.

The night before

No, I'm not mixed up. You know that your day, like every good teacher's day, always begins the night before.

180

Paul was reminding Timothy that a good evangelist and preacher has to be ready to preach at any time, whenever the opportunity is given. However, I'm sure Paul would not disagree with the Teacher who had reminded his readers many years before, that there is a time to be silent and a time to speak (Ecclesiastes 3:7). Before anyone teaches, there must be a time of silence when the necessary preparation can be done. Readiness to teach, like readiness to preach, depends on prior study and planning and prayer. And that takes us to the night before.

Perhaps you don't prepare your day's lessons the night before. Perhaps, as I used to do, you like to prepare a whole week's lessons at one go. I used to try to set aside time at the weekend to plan all my lessons for the following week. That way, I could then see and plan them more clearly as a whole unit with every part hanging together. I didn't always succeed. Many's the time I had to prepare some lessons the night before they were due to be taught.

And many teachers prefer that way. Then they're right up to date, and can incorporate ideas and work that happened the day before, more easily. That would also include all those unplanned things that take place in a teacher's day. It also takes account of the planned things that have had to be left aside for another time.

But you know as well as I do that some teachers, after the first year or so in the profession, don't prepare much. The examples of last year are taken out, dusted down and used again, and again, and again. Often the whole programme is the same as well. I'm not against using good ideas several times. But it's easy to get into a rut as a teacher. After all, this year's eight- or thirteen-year-olds are pretty well at the same stage as last year's. And in every subject there are things that must be taught at just that stage of their development. So it's very easy after a few years to slide into that rut. Then you just groove along. And that's a great way to go stale as a teacher.

So be ready. Because this year's pupils are different from last year's. Not all their needs will be the same. Each lot has its own special ethos, group feeling and response. And whether they wanted to come to school or not, and whether they like your particular subject or not, they expect you to be ready for them, to have something for them which will interest and help them. So be prepared in season and out of season.

Lesson time

So now you're ready to teach. You've got up bright and early of course. You've had your quiet time with the Lord, you've drunk your orange juice and your coffee. You may even have had your bacon and eggs, or cornflakes and toast. So you can't wait to be up and at 'em. And the message is clear. Correct, rebuke, and encourage. Or, if you prefer more of the three Rs, rectify, reprimand, and reinforce. You know only too well that you'll need constantly to employ all three methods, whatever the age of your pupils.

But don't dodge the issue, as some teachers do. Children and young people do need correcting. They surely also need rebuking and reprimanding from time to time, when they misbehave. I had one infant-school teacher on the phone last night. She's just finished the first week of a new term, and was saying how hard it had been, because the children were so much more undisciplined than last year's group at this stage.

However, you don't rebuke a child for not being able to do the work set. So many teachers do that and it's grossly unfair. If children are slow or lacking ability, to slap them down and be angry with them is awful. Most of all they need encouragement. Especially after being corrected and rebuked. Reinforcement to help them further is essential.

And you do all this, Paul says, with great patience and careful instruction. You can tell that Paul knew about teaching. Did you notice that he put 'patience' before 'instruction'? What's more, it's 'great patience' that he stresses – 'all longsuffering', as the King James Version translated it. It's one of the supreme attributes of a good teacher. A very popular quality. But you certainly need a lot of it – often. Teachers are patient because they know the capabilities of their pupils. They hope and expect them to get there in the end. The problem is that some of them take a heck of a lot longer than you want them to.

And you need patience for more than just the students themselves. You need it for the teaching as well. That must be unfailing also.

So I urge you to take good care of yourself. I know you have real concern for your classes. I'm sure you're ready to put up with their problems and learning difficulties, as well as to enjoy them. But you'll be better able to do all that if you don't neglect yourself. So pray much, and apply the Word to your situation.

Break-times

Each day, you'll have times when you have a break from actual teaching. That's when you see most of your colleagues. What are your fellow teachers like? They may well be a pleasant and dedicated bunch. Do they teach 'sound doctrine' as you try to do? I only ever taught full-time in the maintained sector. I had some great colleagues. Many were not Christians, alas, but they worked hard and set a good example. But some taught dubious things sometimes. And they were not averse to attacking Christianity and Christian pupils when they felt like it.

Paul's words in verses 3 and 4 refer to Timothy's hearers. You know there are many pupils who have 'itching ears' to hear unsound things. But you must teach what is true, and resist what is false, sham and adulterated. And you'll have to go on resisting these things in your times out of the classroom as well. You need to 'turn from godless chatter and the opposing ideas of what is falsely called knowledge' (1 Timothy 6:20). I've met plenty of that in my teaching career and I expect you have too. It's not always easy to avoid it, but God will help you to do so positively and with tact.

Duty times

I don't know your situation, obviously, but most teachers have other duties to perform as well as actual teaching. Most of them are responsible for a particular class, so they have to register their attendance, help with individual problems, oversee their work and progress in general, write reports on them all, and so on. There are other duties too. Supervision, organizing subject departments, ordering books and equipment, and setting and marking exams.

Paul told Timothy, 'Keep your head in all situations, endure hardship, do the work of an evangelist, discharge all the duties of your ministry.' If you substitute the word 'teacher' for 'evangelist', you have ideal advice for your daily school life. So don't panic. There *will* be hard times, so hang in there. And carry out *all* your duties. That kind of calmness, endurance and conscientiousness is a great witness to everyone of the love of Jesus.

The business of assessment

Richard Peters, the well-known philosopher of education, once commented that one problem for teachers is that they are both judge and probation officer at the same time. What's for certain is that you are constantly subjecting your students to scrutiny. All the time you're checking on them and their progress, analysing their character development, and testing their ideas and knowledge. This provides a great challenge and tremendous opportunities for you. Because, as a Christian, you will not evaluate as the world does. You'll try to look at each child through the eyes of Christ.

I shall never forget one of the very first experiences I had as a teacher. I'd just started my first week, and I'd completed two days when the head teacher called me into his office. I wondered what I'd done wrong. But all he did was to ask me to give some extra English lessons to a boy who had returned to school to re-take examinations he'd failed the previous summer.

'I didn't want him back,' my head teacher snapped. 'But we've got to have him. He's useless. He's just a corner boy. Do what you can, and make sure he passes, so we can get rid of him for good. He's never been any use to this school, so the sooner we see the back of him for ever the better.'

I escaped from his room as quickly as I could, to go and find the youth. He turned out to be rather a pathetic, weedy-looking sort, not at all what I'd imagined. I felt sorry for him. He'd been described as a 'corner boy' – which meant that he hung around street corners in the evening. Whether he did or not, I've no idea. But I had pictured a real tough.

You'd have felt sorry for him too, if you could have seen him. And if you could have talked with him, you also would have found him not unintelligent, and certainly not the hopeless case he'd been made out to be. His problem was that no-one had ever encouraged him to think he could succeed. So he fulfilled everyone's expectations and failed. The head dismissed him as no use, because all he wanted from the students was that they got as many examination passes as possible. This boy had let the school down.

The reality was not that he was no use to the school, but that the school had been no use to him. What he needed was the restoration of his self-respect. Once he realized that he was not the thickie he'd been branded, he made progress. and did pass his examinations eventually. Not very well. But he passed. Even so, school certainly was not for him 'the happiest days of his life'. He'd been labelled for too long with a bad assessment.

Examinations and tests are only one form of student assessment that you'll have to do. And they're by no means the most important, as my former head thought and lots of teachers and parents certainly still think. Much more significant are personal evaluations. My example just quoted is a clear illustration of that. It's your personal evaluation that will determine your pupils' success and failure in everything they do in school for you. So how do *you* weigh up the young people in your care?

Perhaps it'll help you to recall how the world evaluates them. And that means how some of your fellow teachers sum them up. There are five very common tests that the world applies. We'll glance at each one in turn.

1. Appearance

If you're honest, you'll be influenced by the way your students look. One of my present undergraduate students stands out above just about every other student in Durham. He wears a rose-pink teeshirt under a black leather jacket covered with artificial studs. He usually has extremely tight-fitting dirty jeans which tuck into scuffed cowboy boots. Brightest of all is his hairstyle. He sports a Mohican cut, which changes colour every week. Last week it was pink. The week before it was bright green. Yesterday it was vermilion red.

When I first met him, I didn't think he *was* a student, but someone who'd come into the wrong place by mistake. You see, Durham undergraduates just don't look like that at all. Not ever. For the most part they are really rather tidy and well turned out. Neither do most local youngsters look as my student does. So when I saw him, I admit to you that my heart sank. I'm very sorry about that. I'd automatically labelled him. I responded to the wrapping-paper, and not to the contents of the parcel.

In fact, he's quite a nice chap. He's careless, forgetful, casual about keeping appointments. And his work varies. But he's succeeding. And we expect him to achieve a reasonable degree result at the end of his course. I think what really showed up my first judgment of him were the studs on his clothes. They were made of plastic. They look really vicious. But when he once accidentally brushed against my arm, I realized they were false. Just like his whole appearance. That was saying one thing to all who looked at him. But he isn't really like that at all.

The Lord says; 'Stop judging by mere appearances, and make a right judgment' (John 7:24). So how do you react to your pupils when you see them? Some will be physically attractive. Others will be very plain. A few may even appear ugly. Are the handsome and pretty ones 'good', and the plain and ugly ones 'bad'? The world usually suggests this. Some are small and weak, others are tall and in fine physical shape. Some are dressed neatly. Others are very ill turned out. Which do you respond to most readily? It really is hard not to be influenced by appearances. Your pupils will certainly be swayed by what they see.

2. Intelligence

Most teachers like teaching bright pupils. The rewards are so much more obvious. They're usually easier to teach as well. What happens in your school? When you all meet together, which pupils get the best publicity? On public occasions, how much notice is paid to those who did *not* come out top of the class? How welcome and accepted are *your* slow learners? Or does the praise go only to the able?

I've always been keen on sport, and I used to help with the various school teams. I recall selecting one boy for one of the school football teams, only to have him replaced by the other colleague who helped, and who was senior to me. He rejected my choice because he preferred a cleverer boy. The fact that my choice was the better player was dismissed. 'It will be better all round to have the other,' I was assured. 'There's not much difference between them' (which was true), 'and my choice will be a better advertisement for the school.'

I asked; 'Will it be better all round for the boy I selected?' This remark was ignored.

I still feel sad and angry when I think of the incident. The boy I'd chosen was deeply upset. He knew he was a better player. And I've often wondered what the effect was on the rest of the team. After all, they also knew the boy I'd picked was the better player. An injustice had been done. And all because one teacher had applied the intelligence test in a situation that was inappropriate.

3. Special talents

My story leads naturally on to a third way in which the world values people: success in various activities. I visited a mid-west American school a few years ago. It was a sort of parents' day when pupils performed and their work was displayed. The whole emphasis was on athletic success and the skill of the school orchestra. I've been to English schools where again that sort of success was praised, and nothing at all said about all the many pupils who were not good at games or music.

Have *you* noticed that if it's not the intelligent pupils, then it's the good gymnasts and ball players and athletes who get the attention? Close behind them come those good at music, or art, or dancing, or drama. How would you and your colleagues react if the school music teacher put on a concert in which anyone who wanted to was encouraged to sing, whether they had a good voice or not? How *do* they react when they see the gawky, fat, or puny child in the gym or on the race track? Or when they hear some of the less accomplished readers or instrumentalists?

How do you react? I'm sure you know how God reacts. He looks on the heart. So he judges the intention rather than the quality of the performance.

4. Important connections

Do any of the pupils in your school have parents or other relatives in positions of power? What about the mayor's son or the judge's daughter? Or the children of a leading local business man or politician? Maybe a well-known actor's boy is in your class. Or a pop star's child. How are they treated, compared with the rest? Maybe their parents are school governors. If so, do they have a bigger say than the others? Are they more likely to influence what goes on in school?

There's a real problem there for many schools. And for the pupils concerned.

5. Wealth

Money talks, they say. If you'll allow me to say so, I

think it talks too much these days at all levels of education. Do you recall how James, in chapter 2 of his letter, attacks those who show favouritism? They make a fuss of the rich person who comes to their church, but discriminate against the poor person. I once taught a boy whose father owned a string of radio and television shops. He was extremely rich – and he was generous to the school in a number of ways. The boy was not an able pupil. But I was urged to do my best for him. Well, of course, I would. But why just him? Are the children from Nob Hill more deserving than those from the east side of town? You know the answer as well as I do.

A biblical example

Let's not be self-deceiving about all this. You are under real pressure about assessment. The world will want, and *expect*, you to take due note of its own estimates about what is worthwhile and praiseworthy. Appearance, intelligence, special talents, connections and wealth are the criteria you will be forced to put first, if you're not very careful. They may well be some of the idols of the 'old man' inside you from which the Lord Jesus has delivered you. It's highly likely that your thinking will be automatically coloured by such values. We all need to watch and pray diligently about this.

It's one of the oldest of human problems. Do you remember how the prophet Samuel, for instance, once had to face up to this problem of assessment? Do you recall how the Lord once said to him. 'On your way, Samuel. I've got a job for you. Get yourself over to Bethlehem. There's a man there called Jesse. He's got a lot of sons. I've chosen one to be the new king, and I want you to go to anoint him.'

Samuel was not very keen on the idea, because King Saul was still alive and in control. He'd be likely to harm

Samuel if he found out. But Samuel knew he had no choice, and so he went, trusting the Lord to take care of him.

When he saw Jesse and his sons, he took a really good look. Eliab, the eldest, caught his eye straight away. 'That's the one the Lord sent me to anoint,' he thought. God stepped in at once. Samuel needed straightening out on this assessment problem, just like the rest of us. So God said:

> *Do not consider his appearance or his height, for I have rejected him. The Lord does not look at the things man looks at. Man looks at the outward appearance, but the Lord looks at the heart (1 Samuel 16:7).*

Samuel didn't make a mistake again. He rejected all the sons until David, the youngest, appeared before him. Then God said, 'That's the one.' So he anointed him.

There's your principle. With the Lord's help look at the heart, not at the surface. And help your students to do the same. You'll be performing a great Christian witness if you do, setting a super example, and challenging the world at the very heart of its approach.

One last thought

We send our children to school to learn. There is so much that they need to know to equip them for life. All schools rightly place great value on knowledge. They want their pupils to acquire as much as possible. I'm sure you agree with that. You support that aim. So do I.

But you and I know something that many teachers and education authorities don't know. And it's something they ought to know. It's also something you and I want all our pupils, especially the ablest ones, to understand and come to terms with. It's this:

Knowledge puffs up, but love builds up (1 Corinthians 8:1).

You know, that would make a splendid school motto. It certainly underlines the key principle for every Christian teacher.

Your pupils need knowledge, obviously. They also need love. And they all need more love than knowledge. Knowledge can so easily produce self-importance, even though none of us knows anything yet as we ought to know. Any teacher worth his or her salt can teach children knowledge. The supreme gift of the Christian teacher is knowledge clothed in love.

The knowledge is necessary for their understanding and right conduct. But love is the surer guide, especially where behaviour is concerned. Your pupils depend on you for both. And don't forget that you may be the only adult in their lives who can give them both. But they also need to grasp the true value of both.

One Christian teacher was taking a current affairs lesson. The newspapers were full of a major bullion robbery. He used this story to put across a proper valuation of knowledge and love. He got the class to analyse the knowledge and skills needed by the thieves. They came up with the following list:

- They knew how to plan the theft (organizational skills).
- They knew about the timetables and the value of money (mathematical knowledge).
- They knew how to break into the bullion depot (technical knowledge).
- They knew the layout of the area and where to go to escape (geographical knowledge).

- They were extremely fit (physical education skills).

But all that knowledge was used for selfish ends and to hurt people. The *class* decided that the thieves needed much more moral knowledge 'like in the Sermon on the Mount', so that they would learn to love and be kind to others, and not hurt them. The *class* agreed that character education mattered more than any other kind of knowledge.

When you think of the teacher as teacher, who better than you, a Christian teacher, to provide that moral knowledge?

For prayer and discussion

1. Go through the two letters Paul wrote to Timothy. Make a note of every comment which you think applies to you as a teacher. Build up a character sketch of a Christian teacher from your notes.

2. Read again 1 Corinthians 13. Can you think of examples from your teaching experience where the different characteristics of love did apply, or should have applied? Pray about the examples you thought of.

3. A Christian teacher I know has been strongly criticized by some of his colleagues because, they say, his expectations of his pupils are too high, especially at a time when society is so much more relaxed about standards. Discuss with other Christians how you would answer such a charge today.

11

Perseverance, the teacher's ultimate attribute

I want to begin this chapter with a quotation from one of my favourite authors, John White.

Let me encourage you, then, not to think primarily of success. Should God grant it to you, rejoice and praise him. Your aim is not 'success' in the way the world around you measures success but to please Christ by the way you tackle even unrewarding tasks. Work is not your 'stepping stone' to higher things. It is an act of worship to a Savior (The Fight, IVP, 1977, p. 211).

That's very challenging to any teacher, don't you think? After all, we *are* in the success business, so it seems. The world certainly thinks so. Nearly all parents want their children to do well at school. They expect the teachers to bring this about. So do industry and commerce.

But teachers also want to be successful. You do, don't you? I know I do. No teacher likes to see children fail, and leave school with little to show for their time there. So most of them constantly strive to enable their students to achieve the grades they need. What's more, teachers tend to judge their colleagues by the grade levels and examination successes of their pupils. How often have you heard one teacher comment about another; 'Oh, he's a good teacher. His kids always do well.' Or, 'I'm sorry for that class. They'll never get very far with X.'

I'm not going to complain too much about the fact that society judges its schools on the basis of their academic record. After all, society has a right to expect some academic success from its schools. Like you, I work hard to help my students to do well. But I'm concerned about their personal and social development as well as their academic competence. That's why I'll always argue against the world's insistence on measuring a school's quality solely in terms of the grades that its pupils obtain.

In any case, John White was not suggesting that we should never think of success at all. He just tells us not to put that goal at the top of our list. It's not the Christian's first priority for himself or herself. The Lord Jesus never commanded His disciples to be successful. He gave them the power to succeed, and they did frequently rejoice in achieving what they had been sent out to do. But what he most wants of His people is that they be faithful. Remember the parable of the talents? It was the faithfulness of the servants that their master praised. Christ's words to the church in Smyrna sum it up:

Be faithful, even to the point of death, and I will give you the crown of life (Revelation 2:10).

John White reminds us that our work is an act of worship to the Saviour. Had you ever thought of your teaching like that? It certainly puts each new teaching day into a different perspective, don't you think? Even more, it sheds a different light on everything you do, the unrewarding tasks as well as the attractive ones.

Nevertheless, to be a teacher isn't easy today, as I've said more than once in this book. If you asked me to choose the quality I believe teachers need more than anything, I think I'd choose patience or perseverance. Yes, I know you must love children. I know you must enjoy academic study. I know you need good qualifications and pedagogic skills. But to apply all of these year in, year out, for up to forty years, demands real persistence, especially when you recall the many stresses that the work imposes on all who teach.

Think of your own school days. Which teachers do you remember best? Ask around your friends. See what answer they give to this question. I can virtually guarantee that, if you made a count, the majority of remembered teachers would be those faithful men and women who have been doing the job patiently and caringly for years.

For some peculiar reason, I keep thinking of that lovely Peanuts greetings card. I'm sure you will have seen it. On the front, it has Snoopy on top of his kennel with the legend, 'Love is where you find it.' Open the card and you find the same picture, but this time with the words, 'I'll be here all day.' In a way, that sums up my point. You'll *be* there. And go on being there. It's at the heart of the job.

If you agree with me about the importance of perseverance, then you'll also agree, I hope, that the subject is worth delving into in more detail. What exactly does it involve? What does it mean?

Definition time

1. Perseverance. I begin as usual with my *Concise Oxford Dictionary*. There I learn that perseverance is the 'steadfast pursuit of an aim'. It is 'constant persistance'. It's continuing steadfastly in a course of action, or with a task. So you see it has two main aspects: (a) it's unwavering, and (b) it's constant and on-going. It never stops, not even to take a break.

You'll have spotted that both of them are constructive qualities. There's nothing negative there. The same is true of the other word which most obviously links up with 'perseverance', namely 'patience'. So what does the *Dictionary* say about that?

2. Patience. Patience is 'calm endurance of pain or of any provocation.' It is 'forbearance'. It is 'quiet and self-possessed waiting for something'.

It seems the key marks of a patient person are the ability to bear problems calmly, and the ability to wait without fuss or anxiety. As my old granny used to say, when, as a small boy, I used to get agitated or over-eager about something: 'It'll come, son. Things always come to him who waits.' They didn't always come, I remember, but she was right about being patient.

The Bible's definition

The New Testament also has quite a lot to say on the subject. The Greek word most commonly translated 'perseverance' or 'patience' is *hypomonē*, which literally means 'an abiding under'. Once again a highly positive attribute. And that's hardly surprising, since patience is part of the fruit of the Spirit (Galatians 5:22)

Patience and perseverance, then, are never to be associated with despair or frustration. They do not refer to hopeless resignation to something. They are plus, not minus, factors. They are based on hope. But not everybody realizes that. Have you noticed that, if you tell some people to be patient and keep pressing on, they groan and moan. They think patience means a sort of spiritless endurance of something. You can't change it, so you've just got to grin and bear it. There's no expectancy there. Nothing positive.

But if you really are forbearing, abiding quietly, steadfast and constant, you must have some confidence in the future, as well as determination to see things through for as long as it takes. There's real hope there. And as every Christian knows, or should know, hope is not mere wishful thinking. It's genuine confidence in what is to come. It's when doubt sets in that you lose your cool.

The call to persevere

The letter to the Hebrews says this:

> *Let us run with patience the race marked out for us (Hebrews 12:1).*

Now that's a command to every Christian, not just the Christian teacher. If we succeed, the rewards are great. As Paul reminded the Romans, God will give eternal life to those who, by persistence in doing good, seek glory, honour and immortality (Romans 2:7). But we're all left in no doubt that 'the race' will not be easy. As Jesus told His disciples, 'In this world you will have trouble' (John 16:33).

The faithful Christian, then, is bound to experience suffering wherever he or she lives and works. But that's positive too, if we view it in the Bible way. How? Paul explains like this:

> *We also rejoice in our sufferings, because we know*

198

*that suffering produces perseverance; perseverance,
character; and character, hope (Romans 5:3–4).*

Did you notice? The first fruit of suffering is perseverance. James develops a similar idea in his letter. He
wrote:

*The testing of your faith develops perseverance.
Perseverance must finish its work so that you may
be mature and complete, not lacking anything (James
1:3–4).*

And Peter made the point that we should add to our
faith 'goodness; and to goodness, knowledge; and to
knowledge, self-control; and to self-control, perseverance; and to perseverance godliness, and to godliness,
brotherly kindness; and to brotherly kindness, love' (2
Peter 1:5–7). Why? Because these qualities keep you
from being ineffective and unproductive Christians.

So perseverance is essential for two reasons. First, to
help you to be an effective Christian. Secondly, to help
you towards maturity of character. So your patience is
good for you *and* good for others at the same time. And
that can't be bad, can it?

I remember often hearing, when I was a child, the old
story of the Scottish leader, Robert the Bruce. On the
run from his enemies, he once hid in a cave. While
there, his attention was drawn to a spider trying to spin
its web. It kept making attempts to secure the web and
failing. After many tries, it finally succeeded, teaching
the lesson that if at first you don't succeed, try, try, try
again. Robert the Bruce was given new heart by this
example, and he determined to try again to beat his
enemies. He eventually succeeded, and became king of
Scotland.

I know, but I'm tired

I spend so much of my life with young people aged between nineteen and twenty-three that it's necessary for me to talk with experienced teachers from time to time. You see, it's easy to tell my students to persevere, because they usually nod wisely and accept that they must do this. They don't really know what they're in for, despite the extended practice we give them. But try the same advice on a group of older teachers and you're almost bound to get, from a few at least, a sigh or two, and that weary look which says; 'Yeah, I've heard it all before, but I'm tired'. And I'm talking about Christian teachers. They're human too, you know.

Some years ago I went to a Christian teachers' conference at a centre in Derbyshire, England. I got there the day before I was due to speak, so I could enjoy the fellowship and listen to some of the other speakers. One of them exhorted us to fight the good fight of faith, and he kept quoting Sir Harry Lauder's famous song 'Keep Right on to the End of the Road'.

Afterwards, as we sat over a cup of coffee, I listened to the discussion around me. All the teachers were experienced folk. They were quite critical of the speaker on the grounds that he really had no idea what a teacher's life was like. (He was a university lecturer in theology.) The general view was that what he said was sound, but reality made the difference. Here are the sort of comments they made:

- What he says is all right in theory, but you try to put it into practice. You soon get a bit disillusioned.
- He ought to teach in *our* school.
- He's obviously a good man, but how can he know what life's really like from his ivory tower?
- He doesn't have thirty nine-year-olds yammering at

him all day.
- If I had ten days in every week in school, instead of five, and I was ten years younger, I could do what he says I should do.

I was surprised to hear so many expressions of weariness and disillusionment. For, as I've told you, they were Christian teachers.

Why were they so negative? They had every intention of going back to their schools to work conscientiously as before. But the sparkle I see so often in the eyes of my students was missing. What was wrong?

I've thought about that a number of times. I think it's important to stress that Christian teachers *do* have many of the same problems as their other colleagues. They do get tired and dispirited sometimes. It does not follow that, because they are Christians, they'll sail through every difficulty without undue stress or strain. We do have our treasure in jars of clay, as Paul reminded the Corinthians. So we do fail. We do make mistakes. We do get downhearted and discouraged.

Two Old Testament examples

But we're not the only ones. Do you remember Elijah? James describes him in his letter as 'a man just like us' (James 5:17). He prayed for no rain, and the heavens closed for three and a half years. God fed and cared for him miraculously all that time. Then came the Mount Carmel incident when God demonstrated that 'The Lord – he is God!' The prophets of Baal were routed, and Elijah prayed for rain. And the rains came.

Tremendous. What great and privileged experiences. And then look what happened. Queen Jezebel sent him a message, saying in effect, 'Tomorrow at this time, you'll be just like them.'

How did Elijah react? Did he remind her that it is the Lord who is God? Did he recall his past experiences? Did he even commit the whole matter to God, and wait for Him? You know he did none of these things. The Bible says, 'Elijah was afraid and ran for his life' (1 Kings 19:1).

He was so depressed and discouraged. Suddenly he was weary and sick of the whole thing. 'I have had enough, Lord,' he prayed. 'Take my life.' And he lay down and went to sleep. Eventually the Lord confronted him. He moaned away to God, reminding Him how zealous he'd been, and now he was the only one left and his life was in danger.

How did God react? He made no comment about most of what Elijah had said. He simply gave him some new orders. But he finished by informing Elijah that there were seven thousand others in Israel who had not bowed down to Baal. From Elijah's perspective, all was dark and hopeless. He just didn't know the half of it.

Secondly, do you remember the spies whom Moses sent out at the Lord's command to look over Canaan, the promised land? The Israelites were almost at the end of their journey. They'd seen God provide for all their bodily and spiritual needs. Now twelve of their leaders were to go ahead and check out the land. What an exciting time. Journey's end almost in sight. They could hardly wait for the spies to return.

What report did these twelve leaders give? They said, 'It's a great place. It does flow with milk and honey. But the people who live there are stronger than us. They live in large fortified cities. There are even giants there. We looked like grasshoppers beside them' (cf. Numbers 13:27–33).

Only Caleb and Joshua were positive, putting their trust in God to see them through. But the Bible tell us; 'That night all the people of the community raised their voices and wept aloud' (Numbers 14:1).

Like Elijah and some of those Christian teachers I quoted, they did not accentuate the positive, as the old pop song phrased it. They simply concentrated on the difficulties and their own weaknesses. Their perspective was all wrong. And the result? Not one of the doubters ever set foot in the promised land.

Coming back to the present, there seem to be quite a lot of Christian writers and lecturers who encourage us all to take a very positive stand. (I'm doing that myself, for my sake as well as yours.) They make many useful points, and give us heartwarming illustrations. But I have to say that some of them seem to suggest that it's never too difficult to live victorious Christian lives all the time. They make it sound so easy. All you have to do is avail yourself of the power of Christ. That may well be true. But we still all get tired. And the pressures can become very severe.

So is there no real answer to the question I asked about those teachers I quoted? What *was* wrong? Well, as I've implied, I think they'd got their perspective a little out of focus. They were right to say that the reality of the teaching situation was much more wearing than the speaker had seemed to realize. But they too were not taking account of the full reality of the situation either. They felt the pressures and the tiredness that resulted. They knew that their own resources to meet them were limited. But they were tending to assume that all they had at their disposal was their own expertise. No wonder they became weary.

Getting your perspective right

They needed to take another look at their situation. This time, not from where *they* were sitting but from the eternal standpoint provided for us in Scripture by the Lord.

Don't you find you keep needing to do this? I certainly do. I'm afraid I also look through unfocused lenses from time to time. I find it all too easy to be like Elijah in judging from too blinkered a viewpoint. But the Bible offers a number of passages which help us to widen our vision to take in the whole picture, and not just our restricted bit of it. Here's one such passage. Whenever you feel discouraged or that your work is getting on top of you, remember these verses and allow the priorities they stress to reinforce and redirect your thinking.

I always thank God for you because of his grace given you in Christ Jesus. For in him you have been enriched in every way – in all your speaking and in all your knowledge – because our testimony about Christ was confirmed in you. Therefore you do not lack any spiritual gift as you eagerly wait for our Lord Jesus Christ to be revealed. He will keep you strong to the end, so that you will be blameless on the day of our Lord Jesus Christ. God, who has called you into fellowship with his Son Jesus Christ our Lord, is faithful (1 Corinthians 1:4–9).

Now that you've read it through, look at it again. You'll find it's concerned to emphasize three priorities for anybody with a perseverance problem.

- It picks out an eternal perspective.
- It points up the way to success.
- It provides the reason for assurance.

Whenever you start losing your perspective, the first thing to do is always to re-examine the facts. All the facts. Get them all clear, and you start to see clearly once again. Sometimes this will take time. You need to stop what you're doing, no matter how busy you are, and take stock. Never mind how urgent the demands of the moment seem to be. Sit down and prayerfully review the situation. I know that's easier to say than to do. But you must discipline yourself to do it. After all, what's the good of pressing on when your judgment is out of true? You *must* take fresh note of all the facts. And don't be too shy or too proud to ask other Christians to help you.

An eternal perspective

For the Christian, the facts always begin with God. How does He view you and your situation? What Paul says on this is as true for Christians who teach as it was for the Corinthians he was writing to.

What are the facts, then? First, that you have been given the grace of God in Jesus Christ. Secondly, you have been enriched in every way in all that you know and say. How does that strike you? Enriched in all your knowledge and speaking. Isn't that exactly the teacher's situation? Notice that you have been enriched in *every* way. I know it doesn't always feel like that, but you've never been told to trust your feelings. If God's Word says it, that's good enough. That's all you need. What you have to do is to believe it.

Thirdly, you don't lack any spiritual gift. They are all available for you, to use as needed. Our God is a bountiful God who is able to do immeasurably more than all we ask or imagine (Ephesians 3:20). And He lavishes the riches of His grace upon us (Ephesians 1:7–8). So there you are. Enriched, equipped, and all through grace. But now for an important digression.

The problem of pressure

You say, 'I know and accept all that. Don't think I'm not grateful. I surely am. But sometimes the pressure gets so great. And my pupils make so many demands on me. Sometimes I'm just glad to survive the term. The real trouble is that I'm only human.'

Right. So was Paul. Just think what he had to put up with. He put it like this to the Corinthians:

But we have this treasure in jars of clay to show that this all-surpassing power is from God and not from us (2 Corinthians 4:7).

You and I must never get false ideas about ourselves. You were right. You *are* only human. So, although God has enriched and equipped you fully for your work as a teacher and as a Christian, you'll never do it in your own strength. In fact, it's crucially important that you and everyone else recognize this. It would be fatal for you and your pupils and colleagues if they thought your ability and gifts were solely yours, and that your witness was all from you. *You* know it's not. They need to know it too. Praise God for the jars of clay.

But that means pressure as well. There's no escape from it wherever you teach. Listen to Paul again:

We are hard pressed on every side, but not crushed; perplexed, but not in despair; persecuted, but not abandoned; struck down, but not destroyed. We always carry around in our body the death of Jesus, so that the life of Jesus may also be revealed in our body (2 Corinthians 4:8–10).

You see, more negatives. You're not just a jar of clay. You're a jar of clay with pressures. All sorts of them. You may be hard pressed. You may be perplexed. You may be enduring persecution right now. You may be feeling really struck down.

But there are positives too. Despite the pressure, the perplexities and the persecution, you're not completely crushed. Not in utter despair. Not abandoned. Certainly not destroyed. And by carrying around in your body the death of Jesus, His life is revealed in you. And surely that's what you want people to recognize, more than anything else. I guess Paul suffered more than any of us in his life as a Christian. But the God who sustained him is the same God who upholds and protects and empowers us. So if Paul can emphasize these positives, we can also.

And don't forget the best positive of all. You may be a jar of clay, but you have *treasure* inside you. Treasure of the richest and loveliest kind. You have the indwelling Spirit of God. Your body is a temple of the Holy Spirit.

You'll not avoid pressure and its problems. I think I'd be worried for you if you did. But you *can* cope with all the hassle and the difficulties. You really can. Just remember the facts.

The way to success

Once the facts are clear to you, it becomes easier to see your situation in much more positive terms. You can go back to school tomorrow and next term and next year with a renewed heart. And that's not the end of it. God doesn't just enrich you and equip you and then say; 'Right, now you're on your own. I've given you the ability, so get cracking.' He never just leaves you to it. He points the way to your success by giving you some super promises about the future, for you to hang on to. The passage from 1 Corinthians 1 has one such promise. And it's custom built for the Christian teacher with perseverance problems. Verse 8 says:

He will keep you strong to the end.

You know, there are quite a lot of Scriptures that remind us that 'the Lord is the strength of his people'

(Psalm 28:8). That's no accident. God never repeats Himself unnecessarily. So when we find the same truth again and again in the Bible, we can be sure that God wants us to grasp it firmly. And here is a great promise. He *will* keep you strong to the end. You know you'll never persevere to the end solely in your own strength. Remember those weary Christian teachers at that conference? We can get like that. The Lord knows this only too well.

So He offers you this promise. He *will* keep you strong to the end. He will keep you *strong* to the end. *He* will keep you strong to the end. If you're feeling tense right now about school or a particular class or task you have, doesn't that help where you most need it? It's a promise to claim. And to keep on claiming.

The reason for assurance

Just in case you're so tired that your perspective is still a little askew, even after the facts and the promise, here comes the clincher. It's in verse 9 of that first chapter of 1 Corinthians.

God, who has called you into fellowship with his Son Jesus Christ our Lord, is faithful.

That's it in a nutshell. God is faithful. He who drew you to Christ, who enabled you to have fellowship with the Lord Jesus, is faithful. He promised. He didn't have to, but He did. He promises to keep you strong to the end. So there's no need – and no excuse – for doubt any more. God is faithful.

Doesn't that set your adrenalin flowing again? And make you want to rejoice afresh? And to bow in worship and praise? It puts the problem of perseverance in its true light. It shows you that you *can* claim and exercise the teacher's ultimate attribute. You *can* persevere to the end. Trust in the Lord and He will keep you strong right through all aspects of your life. When you start to wilt, you can still be a winner.

Jesus knew that. He reminded His disciples very plainly that following Him meant taking up the cross daily. It would be hard, and there would certainly be tribulation. But He said: 'Take heart! I have overcome the world' (John 16:33). All you are doing is following in His footsteps. And whatever your situation, you will find, as Jesus Himself did, that God is faithful. Once again, 'Hallelujah!'

For prayer and discussion

1. Look up 2 Thessalonians 3:1–5. Paul wrote that after he'd already written the words in 1:3–5 of the same letter. Meditate on all these verses and especially on the perseverance of Christ.

2. Re-read the story of Elijah in 1 Kings 18 and 19. Concentrate on what God says and does. Is there an application to your own circumstances?

3. Pray for your colleagues in the light of what you know of the problems and pressures each of them faces at school.

4. Look up the word 'patience' in a Bible concordance, and compare the verses where the word is used with the scriptural teaching quoted in this chapter. What practical new insights do they add to your understanding of the term?

12

Education for transformation

Another school year was coming to an end. A Christian teacher friend of mine was wrestling with the problem of final gradings. One pupil caused her much heartache. She knew he expected a grade 'A' from her. She also knew he needed an 'A' in connection with a job he was applying for. He was quite an able pupil, but he was lazy in her classes, and not very co-operative. On merit, he deserved a 'D' grading. And that's what she gave him.

When he learned what his grade was, he was furious. He objected violently, swore at her and was generally disruptive. So she eventually sent him to the head, who offered him the choice of three extra days' work (which would not lead to any change of grade) or a beating. He chose the beating, and was told to apologize to the teacher. He did so with a bad grace, and left the school.

Two years later, his sister warned my friend that he was coming back to school to see her. He said he had some unfinished business to attend to with her. My friend, remembering the last encounter, was a bit scared, not knowing what was to come. Naturally, she prayed about it, and waited.

At the end of one afternoon school, he appeared in the doorway of her room. He marched up to where she was sitting at her desk. Towering over her, he said: 'Two years ago, thanks to you, I got a beating. I was also forced to apologize to you. I didn't want the beating, and I certainly didn't want to apologize. I only did it because I had to.' He paused and took a deep breath.

'I've come now to apologize again, because this time I want to. You were always strict but fair. You always set us good standards. I was wrong and you were right. I knew it, but I was mad at you for costing me a job I wanted. I knew you did what was right because you're a Christian. Well, so am I. I was converted recently, and I remembered you and wanted to put things right between us. That's why I've come back to see you.'

As my friend remarked, 'I could have hugged and kissed him.'

I like that story. I hope you like it too. It's just one more example of what the power and love of God can do to change a life from one of fecklessness to responsibility. And what a change.

The age of Ichabod

It's that kind of change that we urgently need in our schools. I do not know what things are like in your particular school right now, but I'm sure you know they're not good in many of the schools of our country. I've never known a time when teacher morale was so low. There is so much downright discontent. It seems to be everywhere. Grumble, grumble, grumble all round the place.

Many years ago I wrote an article for the Christian journal *Spectrum* on the current state of education. I titled it *Education for Ichabod* because it seemed to me that teaching, and even education itself, had lost its vision. The glory had departed. Sad to say, things have deteriorated further since then.

Of course good teaching continues. Of course many teachers still do a marvellous job every day. But when morale is low, you know how much harder it is to be enthusiastic. You seem to have to make so much more effort to achieve anything. And there isn't the same willingness to help, especially with the unpopular jobs.

Christian teachers are bound to be affected by this mood. There's no escape from it, whether you teach five-year-olds or fifteen-year-olds. So what can they do about it? God in His mercy has placed a great many Christian teachers in the schools of our nation. They are there for just such a time as this, when the mood is negative and standards are slipping. It is their prayerful witness that God will use to bring about the needed changes.

You may think that's a tall order for you. But you're not alone, as God reminded Elijah. And look what happened when he prayed. So what can *you* do about the situation?

I hope you'll agree that what I've written so far does help to answer my question to you. I very much want you to think that it's relevant, and not just some fine-sounding Christian theory which has no real-life application to your teaching situation. What I've written is about witnessing to Christ in the classroom – your classroom. For that's what the education scene most needs today. Faithful, dedicated, determined Christian example.

Christian teacher, your colleagues and your pupils

need you today more than they have ever done before. That's as true of Britain as it has ever been. It's true for other countries also. So I urge you with all my heart to apply the scriptural truths we've been examining in this book to *your* school and *your* classroom. And to yourself as a teacher.

But your task does not stop there. For you too need changing. Not like the pupil in the story I've just related to you. That change has already happened if you're a Christian. But what began at your conversion must continue. 'How?' you ask me. 'And how will it relate to my teaching life?'

That question bears heavily on this final chapter. I have thought and prayed much about how I should end this book, and what should be the last scriptures that I leave with you. I have no doubt about the answer, especially if you are faced with depression and discontent in your school; if, for you and your colleagues, the glory has departed. I draw your attention principally to two verses in Paul's letter to the Romans, to which I myself return again and again. Here they are. Let's examine them briefly together.

Therefore, I urge you, brothers [and sisters] in view of God's mercy, to offer your bodies as living sacrifices, holy and pleasing to God – this is your spiritual act of worship. Do not conform any longer to the pattern of this world, but be transformed by the renewing of your mind. Then you will be able to test and approve what God's will is – his good, pleasing and perfect will (Romans 12:1-2).

I'll concentrate on verse 2. It sets up very clearly indeed the challenge that faces you. To conform or to be transformed. There's no alternative. You do either one or the other. You just cannot sit on the fence. That's

213

impossible. So which is it to be? The more you meditate on these two verses, the more sure I am of your answer.

The conformity problem

Let's consider what conforming means, first. After all, we live in an age of conformity. To conform means to mould oneself in the likeness of someone or something else. It means to keep in step with everyone else; to jump on, and stay on, the bandwagon; to swim with the tide; to do as others do. The Greek word that Paul uses – *syschēmatizō* – literally means 'to fashion in the same way'. You and I know only too well the compelling power of fashion in our day, in all areas of life.

The pressures to conform today are powerful indeed. And did you notice that the emphasis in Romans 12:2 is upon *your* doing the conforming? It's not someone else moulding and shaping you like the potter shaping his clay. *You* do the conforming. And the words apply to young and old alike.

I have conducted a number of research studies among teenagers. In particular, I have concentrated on the development of their moral attitudes. On issues like telling lies, putting self first, hating, coveting, sexual relations out of marriage, and disobedience to parents and the law, the two most common justifications they put forward for their views and actions were 'It's only natural', and 'Everybody does it.' So they believe conforming is both right and essential to keep the approval of their friends.

What about adults? They're just as bad. They must keep up with the Joneses, or follow the way of the in-crowd or their own social set. After all, what would the neighbours think if they didn't? Christians are no more immune from this than anyone else. If you raise your arms when singing in some churches, you'll get some very funny looks. And if you don't raise them in other churches, the same looks come your way.

What about Christian teachers? I know a lot of Christian teachers in Britain and in America who would readily say that Romans 12:1–2 clearly applies to their lives as Christians, but not to education. At least, they'll not actually *say* that, if you challenge them, but their practice says it. What do I mean? Well, simply this. They'll strive not to conform to the world in their Christian living. But where education is concerned, where do they go for instruction? To the Bible? To Christian writers? Not at all. They go only to the educational experts. And most of them are secular humanists. Yet it's *their* expertise, their ideas, theories, and strategies, that these Christians learn for their work as teachers.

They seem to accept without question that these high-powered educational philosophers and psychologists have all the answers any teacher needs. After all, haven't they done all the research? Haven't they written all these learned books and articles? Don't they produce the teaching texts and materials that most teachers don't have the time to research and prepare for themselves? So they must know best.

And so I find that many Christian teachers conform because they refuse to think Christianly about education. And about how they are to teach. And about the nature and needs of their pupils.

And yet Paul says categorically, 'Do not conform any longer to the pattern of this world.' I'm not for a minute suggesting that secular writers and speakers do not have many good and insightful things to say about teaching and children. But their basic assumptions are godless, and of this world. Christians must challenge them at these points. And they'll do that best by living out their Christian faith in the classroom, by bringing Christian understanding and ways of behaving into their schools.

The pattern of this world

But what is the pattern of this age? You know it is the mass view. What society says. Or what the state determines. The values and standards of this world. The organization person. The advertising person. The rational secular person. All very plausible. All highly insidious. All very appealing. And so often extremely reasonable. Take, for instance, the need to be tolerant. Teachers are increasingly told not to be too dogmatic, but to encourage children and young people to be lenient to others becauses everyone has a right to his or her own view.

What about the importance of sincerity? Nowadays the great test of a person's quality is whether he is sincere in what he says and does. If he's sincere, he must be genuine, and that's all OK. It does not seem to matter whether he's right or wrong, or whether his beliefs are true or false. After all, we mustn't be too harsh. He means well, and that's sufficient.

Teachers, of course, must follow the educational tide. As each new educational theory gains popularity, or some research backing, so the schools must adopt it until the next one comes along. So discipline is relaxed because saying 'No' to children 'inhibits their development'. Or 'We use only discussion methods because all students have a democratic right to their own point of view.' And so on. Not to worry. In a year or two's time, some other theory of learning will hold sway. And then we'll all adapt to that idea.

You may well feel that it's easy to criticize these things, but they are hard to resist. And how can the individual stand against mistaken ideas and dubious teaching methods? Paul has the answer. Back to Romans 12:2. The negative has been tackled. Do not conform. Now for the positive.

The call to transformation

Be transformed by the renewing of your mind. What does that mean? The Greek word is *metamorphoō* – 'to change into another form'. It differs from conforming in two very significant ways. Let's go back to conforming again for a minute. Have you ever seen an actor putting on his make-up? Or a clown preparing for his act in the circus ring? They daub on the greasepaint, put on the wig, add a false nose, and pad out the cheeks and the body. So they look the part. But inside they are the same person. The change is outward, and they have effected it.

Now I know that conforming to the pattern of this world goes much deeper than that. But it is in large measure the outside influences and pressures that mould the person into the required likeness, like pressing a piece of putty or Plasticine till it assumes the shape you want. The individual co-operates willingly with this process for the most part, until outward appearance and inward thought and character are at one. It is like some actors and actresses who have played parts for so long that they can no longer be their natural selves any more. Life has become for them one long act.

Transforming is just the opposite. It's not a change from the outside going inward, but a change from the inside coming out. When you are transformed, your essential Christian nature gradually shows itself on the outside.

I am reminded of a helpful illustration which Jamie Buckingham gave in his book *Risky Living* (Logos International, 1976, chapter 3). He described himself as like a lake, smooth and serene on the surface, but with lots of mud down at the bottom. When criticized, attacked or offended in some way, up comes the mud to the surface. He stresses the need for inner healing and cleansing, so that one becomes a transparent Christian, and the inner purity matches the outer surface. He wasn't talking about transformation so much as the inner reality of his nature showing itself from time to time for what it was. But the idea is relevant.

The transforming Paul refers to, includes that inner cleansing so that the holy God, who dwells in every Christian by the Holy Spirit, shines through in the new creature that the Christian has become. The true inner self of the born-again believer reveals itself in all its loveliness. Jamie Buckingham's problem was that people thought he was a charming, good man, whereas he knew that he was nothing of the sort. It's a problem we all share. But Paul wants the new Christ-likeness that the Holy Spirit imparts in every believer so to affect us that it shows itself openly in all we say and do.

Do you want the most exciting illustration of this? You've probably guessed already. Yes, it is the Lord Jesus Himself. Do you recall how He once took four of His disciples up the mountain with Him, and was transfigured before them? (You'll find the story in Matthew 17, Mark 9, and Luke 9.) His true inner self showed through – and they were blinded by the light of His purity and glory. But that's what Paul is telling us to be. To be transformed, transfigured. There's a thought for you.

You'll recall I said that conforming differed from being transformed in two ways. If you look again at the second verse of Romans 12 you'll see what the second way is. Do not conform, but be transformed. See the difference? *You* do the conforming – which, incidentally, implies that you don't have to, if you don't want to. But you don't do the transforming. It says, *be* transformed. You can't do that yourself. God does the transforming of every Christian. He will mould and shape you into the likeness of His Son. Nevertheless, you do have a part to play. God in His mercy encourages you to cooperate with Him. He never mass-produces Christians from His own production line. They are all individual creations.

The metamorphosis process

You will be transformed by the remaking – the making new – of your mind. That has to be a daily process. It means submitting every day to the Lordship of Christ, coming to Him and allowing Him to work upon and in you to transform your mind and will (the word *nous* includes both mind and will). Both, as you well know, need renewing every day.

You see how important that is for the teacher. Yes, I know it's vital for every Christian. But Christian teachers are revealing their minds to children every day. And if change for the better is to come about, then it will come only through renewed minds who bring out into the open, by word and action, the truth, the love and the righteousness of God.

And what does Scripture tell us that this daily renewing will do for you? What is the outcome of the transformation God is effecting in your life? Back to verse 2 again: 'Then you will be able to test and approve what God's will is – his good, pleasing and perfect will.'

There's your answer. You – yes, ordinary, insignificant, weak, timid, uncertain you, and I, will be certain of God's will for us each day. We shall know it and be able to test it in action. Isn't that tremendous?

God wants you to be like Jesus. He knows exactly what you are like, and He thinks you are special. You are the apple of His eye. He has already given you the mind of Christ (1 Corinthians 2:16). He wants you to allow His mind to shine through you every day. He wants you to be transfigured daily for your pupils' sake, and for His glory.

Transformation in education

You know, the world believes that education can bring about the changes it needs to make the utopia so many people desire. For well over a hundred years, scholars, writers, philosophers and politicians have argued that better education is the answer to the world's problems. They have urged that if people understand, if they know, they will behave more responsibly and more compassionately. This is what so many genuinely believe. You have teenage behaviour problems? Teach them more moral education. You have a drugs problem? Educate people to understand the effects. You have parent problems? Teach the kids at school the skills they need to make them better parents when their turn comes.

It's very sad, isn't it? But Christians know better. They know education may help. It's vital if mankind is to obey the creation mandate to subdue the earth and have dominion over every living thing. It may even help prepare for the Christian message and way of life. But in itself it lacks the *power* to do what the world longs for it to do. Only Christ can supply that power. And He does it through His Holy Spirit, using Christian teachers as one of the chief channels – through their reconciling witness to Himself.

How then can transformation in education take place? It is worth saying again that what you teach is crucial. You do need to surround your pupils with all that is true, honourable, just, pure, lovely, excellent, gracious and praiseworthy. You do need to prepare their minds and protect their spirits by helping them to ponder, meditate on and explore 'these things'.

Your methods must be God-centred too. Transformation requires willingness. You must want to be transformed, and to be open to God in this work. That means self-denial, readiness, and conviction. And for your pupils, it means training in these qualities, and applying the biblical principles of discipline to bring pupils to a state of willingness to learn, and to be changed. In doing this, *you* know you are preparing them for openness to much more than just what we teach them. They are being made ready for the Lord.

For as your pupils commit themselves to the knowledge and skills you teach them, so they will be better able to understand the need for commitment to Christ, when that challenge eventually comes to them.

Conclusion

'Therefore, I urge you, . . . in view of God's mercy, to offer your bodies as living sacrifices, holy and pleasing to God – this is your spiritual act of worship.' This is a daily task as well, for you and me. And if there is still within you the tiniest shadow of a doubt about yourself as you go out tomorrow and the next day to witness for Christ in your classroom, then remember what Paul said to Timothy, who was also rather fearful. He reminded Timothy that God never sends anyone out unequipped into the world to serve Him.

You, like Timothy, have been given the same help, the same ability to do your work for the Lord each day. For, as with Timothy, God has not given you a spirit of timidity, but a spirit of power, of love, and of self-discipline (2 Timothy 1:7). You have the power you need to do all you have to do. You have the love you need to give to your pupils and your colleagues. And you have the self-control to keep yourself pure and unspotted from the world, and to do and say what is right and true each day, in all the situations you'll have to face.

Do you recall something I quoted from a Christian

teacher right at the start of this book? He said, 'We used to think we were taking the Lord with us into school' (which they were). 'Now we know He's there already, and we just have to follow him in there.' As I finish this book, I'd like to quote another Christian teacher who was asked by the publishers to read the typescript of this book before they agreed to publish it. It's a vivid illustration of education for transformation. She said:

Christ dwells not just in the Christian teacher, but His beauty is there already somewhere in the dingy classroom, somewhere in that pile of scruffy exercise books, in the alcoholic colleague and the obscene pupil. As we remember that, teaching becomes again the adventure it ought to be, the daily rediscovery of our Lord in every part of life around us.

With all this in mind, therefore, let us constantly pray 'that our God may count you worthy of his calling, and that by his power he may fulfil every good purpose of yours and every act prompted by your faith. We pray this so that the name of our Lord Jesus Christ may be glorified in you, and you in him, according to the grace of our God and the Lord Jesus Christ' (2 Thessalonians 1:11–12).